A GUIDE TO GENESIS

The SPCK International Study Guides incorporate the much loved and respected TEF series, and follow the tradition of clarity and simplicity; a worldwide, ecumenical perspective; and an emphasis on application of the material studied, drawing out its relevance for Christians today. The Guides are ideal for students and Bible study groups, as well as for multi-cultural classes, and students for whom English is a second language.

SPCK International Study Guide 3

A GUIDE TO GENESIS

John Hargreaves

First published in Great Britain 1969
Society for Promoting Christian Knowledge
Holy Trinity Church
Marylebone Road London NW1 4DU

Second edition 1998
Second impression 1999

ACKNOWLEDGEMENTS
The photographs in this book are reproduced by courtesy of Christian
Aid (p. 80), CMS (p. 148), Mullard Space Science Laboratory (p. 6),
Oxfam/Mike Wells (pp. 14, 80), USPG (p. 64). The map on p. 79
is reproduced by permission of Lutterworth Press.

NOTE ON VERSIONS OF THE BIBLE USED IN THIS BOOK
The English translation of the Bible used in the Guide is the
Revised Standard Version Common Bible Ecumenical Edition (RSV)
copyright © 1952 and 1971. Other translations used
in a few cases where they show the meaning more clearly are
the *New Revised Standard Version* (NRSV) copyright © 1989,
the *New International Version* (NIV) copyright © 1973, 1978, 1984
by the International Bible Society and published by Hodder & Stoughton,
The Revised English Bible (REB) copyright © 1989 Oxford and
Cambridge University Presses, and the *Good News Bible* (GNB)
published by The Bible Societies/HarperCollins Publishers Ltd UK
copyright © American Bible Society, 1966, 1971, 1976, 1992.
The Authorized Version (AV), the text of which is the property
of the Crown in perpetuity, is also mentioned.

British Library Cataloguing-in-Publication Data
A catalogue record of this book is available from
the British Library

ISBN 0–281–05155–0

Typeset by Wilmaset Ltd, Birkenhead, Wirral
Printed in the United Kingdom
at the University Press, Cambridge

Contents

Foreword

The Bible is not a book but a library. It contains many different kinds of writing: poetry and prose, powerful story and detailed history, laws and letters. As part of our respect for scripture we must always be careful to make sure we understand the nature of the chapter that we are currently reading. Otherwise we shall not be able to interpret it correctly. Perhaps no book of the Bible contains a greater variety of material than the Book of Genesis. There is profound theological reflection on the nature of creation (nothing exists but by the will of God alone) and on the human predicament of sinful alienation from the One who is the ground of our being. There is primeval story and the history of the Patriarchs, beginning with the towering figure of Abraham. We shall never be able to understand either Israel or Christianity adequately without a proper understanding of Genesis.

I believe that John Hargreaves has provided an excellent aid to the study of the first book of the Bible. He is careful to represent various different points of view in a fair manner where there are differences of Christian opinion about the character and interpretation of some of the material. As a scientist-theologian, I am particularly grateful for the concise and helpful summaries of issues concerning the relation of scientific understanding to the early chapters of Genesis. I am happy to commend this study guide to those who wish to engage with this important part of scripture.

JOHN POLKINGHORNE

Preface

Some years ago I was asked by a group of Christians to write something about the Book of Genesis. They were studying it seriously, but were finding that it was difficult to interpret and that it led to controversy. So I had a wonderful time re-reading it and discovering how important it was for our lives. In the end the World Council of Churches published what I wrote as part of their 'TEF' programme, and it seems to have been well used in various parts of the world.

But that was thirty years ago! The world has changed in so many ways since then. To give only a few examples: scientists have made new discoveries about the origin of the universe, the huge Russian empire has broken up, the position of women is now very different, we are now even more dangerously misusing the earth and polluting it, easy communication between different people is now widespread. So a very different book is needed. After meeting with groups of lay-workers and consulting experts, I have very largely re-written the original.

I am extremely grateful to those on whose help I have depended: four scientists and theologians who gave special help with chapters 1—3, the Revd Dr John Polkinghorne, Professor Sam Berry the geneticist, Bishop Dr John Taylor, and the Revd Dr Richard Coggins; the Revd David Hinson who read and made suggestions on the whole book out of his experience in Kenya; my brother Cecil, formerly of Bishop's College, Calcutta; Dr Martyn Cundy; my very old friend Canon Gervase Markham; Denise Moll of New Leaf Enterprise, who typed the whole book beautifully; Daphne Terry who for over thirty-five years has shared her unique skills and understanding; and my wife Diana, who might often have complained that I was more interested in Genesis than in her, but never has.

Finally, I want to thank Dr Polkinghorne very much for generously contributing the Foreword.

JOHN HARGREAVES

Using this Guide

Before using this Guide, readers may find it helpful to decide how much of it they plan to use. Half the book is a guide to the first eleven chapters of Genesis, because it is in these chapters that we meet profound truths concerning the relationship between God and human beings. A careful study of these truths is needed in order to understand the rest of the Bible, including the Gospels themselves. If time is short, therefore, some people may think it better to study these eleven chapters in detail, rather than to try to study the whole of Genesis in the same time. Others, however, may want to put aside more time in order to include a study of the important stories of Abraham, Isaac, Jacob, and Joseph.

Each section of this Guide consists of:

> an Outline of the Bible passage,
> an Interpretation of the passage,
> some Notes on special verses, and
> Questions.

In the Outline the Bible passage is retold very briefly in such a way as to make clear certain parts of it. But reading this Outline should not take the place of reading the actual passage in the Bible. We need to read carefully the words of the Bible itself at every stage of our study.

Special Notes

These five Notes are separate from the sections dealing with the Bible passages, partly because of their length, and partly because each concerns more than one section. But if readers find that these Special Notes raise questions which they themselves are not asking, they are free not to study them further.

Questions

Questions for study appear at the end of each section, and at the end of each Special Note. They have been included in order to help readers who are working alone to study more thoroughly, and also to provide work which a group of students could do together. They are of four kinds:

1. The *Word* questions are intended to help readers to check their knowledge of some important words.

2. The *Content* questions are intended to help them check their grasp of the ideas and points of teaching given.

3. The *Bible* questions will help them to compare such teaching with teaching found in other parts of the Bible.

4. The *Application* questions are intended to help readers to think out the practical applications of the Book of Genesis to everyday life. These may be especially suitable for use by a group.

Three other points should be noticed:

(a) These questions are only *suggestions*. Some readers will not want to use them. Other students or a group of students may want to use some of them. Others may want to use them all.

(b) The best way to use these questions is: *first* to read the Bible passage itself, *secondly* to read the relevant section of the Guide over carefully once or twice, and *lastly* to do the work suggested, when possible in writing, without looking at the Guide except when it is stated that the reader should do so.

(c) There is a *Key* at the end of the book so that readers may check their own work on those questions which can be checked in this way (p. 164).

Additional Notes

There are Additional Notes on twenty important words used in the Book of Genesis, to help readers to understand how writers use them here and elsewhere in the Bible (pp. 153–163).

Index

The Index includes only the more important proper names of people and places, and the main subjects which occur in the Book of Genesis or which are discussed in the Study Guide.

Further Reading

GENESIS CHAPTERS 1—50

D. Kidner, *Genesis* (commentary) (Tyndale, 1971)
W. Neil, *One Volume Bible Commentary* (Hodder, 1973)
G. von Rad, *Genesis* (advanced) (SCM, 1979)

GENESIS CHAPTERS 1—11

D. Atkinson, *The Message of Genesis* (Inter Varsity Press, 1990)
N. Carr, *The Origins and Purpose of Life* (BRF, 1993)
J. Gibson, *Genesis 1—11* (St Andrew Press, 1982)
A. Phillips, *Lower than the Angels* (BRF, 1996)
J. Rogerson, *Genesis 1—11* (Sheffield Academic Press, 1991)

THEOLOGIANS AND SCIENTISTS

J. Brooks, *The Origins of Life* (Lion, 1985)
R. Holder, *Nothing but Atoms and Molecules* (Monarch, 1993)
A. Peacocke, *Creation and the World of Science* (OUP, 1979)
J. Polkinghorne, *One World* (SPCK, 1986)
J. Polkinghorne, *Science and Creation* (SPCK, 1988)
J. Polkinghorne, *Science and Providence* (SPCK, 1989)
A. Tilby, *Science and the Soul* (BBC, 1992)
D. Wilkinson, *God, the Big Bang, and Stephen Hawking* (Monarch, 1996)

CARING FOR THE EARTH

Ian Bradley, *God Is Green* (Darton, Longman and Todd, 1990)
E. Echlin, *The Christian Green Heritage* (Grove, 1990)
S. McDonagh, *To Care for the Earth* (Chapman, 1994)
S. McDonagh, *The Greening of the Church* (Chapman, 1990)

HISTORY

D. Hinson, *The Books of the Old Testament* (SPCK, 1992)
D. Hinson, *The History of Israel* (SPCK, 1990)

Introduction
The Book of Genesis

THE AUTHORS

The Book of Genesis seems to have arisen out of the songs and poems in which Israelites recited the experiences of their people. They did this during the many years when the people of Israel were wandering in the wilderness. These songs and stories were not written down, but they were remembered and passed down to later generations. Then, much later, probably between 950 BC and 550 BC, editors collected together many of these songs and stories. But, as they made their collections, they also interpreted the traditions out of their firm belief that God Himself had been guiding, judging and providing for the Israelites. These were the editors and interpreters through whom God speaks to us today. See Special Note B, The Writers of Genesis, p. 40. In later times Jews believed that Moses had personally drawn up laws for the Israelites, so they came to think that he was the author of Genesis and of the other books of the Pentateuch (the first five books of the Bible). But modern Jews point out that we do not read in Genesis itself that Moses was its author, and that in Deut. 34.5 the author records Moses' death.

ITS NAME

'Genesis' is a Greek work meaning 'birth' or 'beginnings'. Those who translated the Old Testament books out of Hebrew into Greek between 250 BC and 100 BC chose this word as the title of the whole book. They did this because the book begins with the Hebrew words for 'in the beginning'. But, as we shall see in the following paragraph, the message of Genesis is much wider than the truth that God 'began' the world.

THE TWO PARTS OF GENESIS

A helpful way to begin a study of Genesis is to notice that it has two parts, Genesis 1—11, and Genesis 12—50. These two parts are different in the following ways:

1. In Genesis 1—11 we are reading about all humanity. The name 'Adam' stands for all of us humans. God created all of us so that we should care for His creation and for one another. But we all fail to do this, and we all need renewal. We all belong together. This is an important truth today when in many parts of the world one group declares that another group has no right to exist. But in Genesis 12—50,

although they contain a message for everyone, the writers mainly tell us about Abraham and his Israelite descendants. The theme is the special 'covenant' or agreement which God had with the Israelites and His purpose for them and how He saved and provided for them.

2. In Genesis 1—11 we see God mainly as the Creator. In Genesis 12—50 the writers show Him as Saviour and Provider. We need both parts of Genesis, because God is more than Creator.

3. In Genesis 1—11 the writers do in some way refer to things which happened but their chief aim was to declare great spiritual truths in poetical language. In Genesis 12—50 the writers had great truths to proclaim, but they aimed to record historical events.

Note: Concerning these 'historical events', scholars are not in agreement. For example, some say that the editors lived so long after the events which they describe that the chapters contain the editors' interpretations rather than reliable history. Others say that because of recent archaeological discoveries (and for other reasons) they believe that the chapters refer to some historical events. See Special Note C, The Two Parts of Genesis, p. 78.

OTHER OPINIONS ABOUT GENESIS

We cannot know all that people have said about Genesis ever since it was compiled. But the following are some of the opinions which Christian theologians and other scholars have held during the last 2000 years.

Some have regarded Gen. 2 and 3 as more important than the rest of the book, because there we learn of the sinfulness of human beings and our need to be forgiven and redeemed. But this theme is not found only in Gen. 2 and 3: it is the main message of all Gen. 2—11, See for example 11.4a and 6.

But perhaps even more scholars have, over the centuries, concentrated on matters arising from Gen. 1. Their opinions have been very varied, and are still very different from each other today, as the following examples show.

Origen of Egypt (185–254) and Augustine of North Africa (354–430) thought about the sort of writing which the authors of Genesis were engaged in. They said that Genesis refers to real historical events, but that we discover its most important message by seeing the events as 'allegories' or 'pictorial illustrations of spiritual truth'. Some Christians were troubled by this and unwisely declared that Origen and Augustine were treating Genesis as 'untrue'.

Copernicus of Poland (1473–1543) and Galileo of Italy (1564–1642) examined stars through their telescopes and discovered that the earth moves round the sun. Many Christians, having read Genesis 1, thought that God made the earth the centre of the universe, and that the sun therefore moves round the earth. So they condemned these scientists for teaching something different from the Bible. Today Christians are learning not to criticize scientists until they have understood them. Most people today agree that those scientists were right about the movement of the earth.

Charles Darwin of England (1809–1882) produced his book *The Origin of Species* in 1859. In it he said that human beings and monkeys had both 'developed' or 'evolved' from the same sort of creature. Many Christians felt that this contradicted Gen. 1.27, in which it seems that God created human beings as completely different from animals. Darwin also said that the 'development' or 'evolution' happened of itself. So he seemed to be saying that there was no creator. Today, although all Christians do not agree on this subject, many feel that God's creation was even more wonderful if He created creatures which could 'evolve' and remake themselves than if He had made them fixed and unchangeable.

THE TWENTIETH CENTURY

During the twentieth century scientists have made many great discoveries. As a result many people have begun to think that scientific study is the only real source of knowledge, and that nothing is true except what scientists can prove. This is the reason why many Westerners do not pay attention to Genesis or to the rest of the Bible. But in fact we find in Genesis and in the rest of the Bible truths which we urgently need, and which scientists cannot provide as part of their special work. For example, scientists can make discoveries without showing what are the right and wrong ways of using them. According to Gen. 2.15 we must 'care for the earth' in order to live on it. We have to learn the right way to use it. Now that scientists have discovered nuclear energy and many new powerful drugs, we very urgently need guidance as to their right use.

Because of these scientific discoveries, biblical scholars are now interpreting Genesis with reference to the use and misuse of the environment (see pp. 13 and 15). Unlike earlier scholars they are also referring to the position of women (see pp. 15–17, 28–31, 34, 37, 38 and 119), and to those who work for the liberation of the oppressed (see p. 144).

OUR USE OF GENESIS

There are three important steps to take if we are to make the best use of Genesis.

First, we must look for the sort of information which Genesis exists to provide. There are many books on such subjects as chemistry and geography, and we need them. But those who have given us Genesis have provided us with a different sort of knowledge. They answer such questions as, 'What sort of God is our God?' and 'How can we live the sort of life which God has planned for us to live?'

Second, we need to study the basic answer which they give. This answer is twofold, and it is repeated throughout the whole Book of Genesis, but especially in the first eleven chapters. It is:

● that God loves His creation and us, His great human family ('His steadfast love' (32.10)) and that He works actively in it and in us for our good;

● that we continually behave as if we had no other authority except ourselves ('being like God Himself', 2.17), but that in truth our welfare and happiness depend on our accepting God's supreme authority.

The third important step is to make our own response.

Questions on the Introduction

1. When editors began to write the Book of Genesis, where did they obtain their information?

2. Give one important way in which Gen. 1—11 are different from Gen. 12—50.

3. Explain in each case why Christians accused the following of giving false teaching: (a) Augustine (b) Copernicus (c) Darwin.

4. Why do we need theologians as well as scientists?

5. What steps should we take in order to make the best use of Genesis?

THE BOOK OF GENESIS
PART 1

1.1—2.4a
In the Beginning, God

OUTLINE

1.1: In the beginning God.
1.2–5: God creates light.
1.6–8: God creates sky.
1.9–13: God separates dry land from water and creates vegetation.
1.14–19: God creates sun, moon and stars.
1.20–3: God creates birds and fish.
1.24–5: God creates animals.
1.26–30 God creates human beings.
1.31—2.4a: Conclusion.

INTERPRETATION

In the first chapter of Genesis we read about the universe which God
has created. If readers want to understand the universe and to have a
right attitude to it, they need to learn from many different sorts of
thinkers. They need especially to learn from theologians and from
scientists. See Special Note A, Theologians and Scientists, pp. 20–22.

This chapter of Genesis was written by theologians under God's
guidance. They were Hebrew priests and they probably wrote it while
the Hebrews were in exile in the advanced civilization of Babylon, after
the Babylonians had conquered them (or perhaps they wrote it just after
the Exile). Their chief aim was to preserve and pass on their knowledge
about God which He had revealed afresh to them through the ideas
which they had gained from earlier generations.

At first sight the chapter seems to be a history of the beginning of the
world. It does indeed refer to an event which actually happened, i.e. the
universe had a beginning. But it is really more like a hymn or poem
than a history. The writers may have based the chapter on Psalm 104,
with which we should compare it. Those who composed that psalm and
this chapter were providing words of worship, like the author of
Revelation 4 many centuries later. They wrote it so that all who read it
should bow before God's majesty. Several phrases are repeated and for

Hubble Deep Field
Hubble Space Telescope · WFPC2

'God created the heavens' (Gen. 1.1). The Hubble Space Telescope took this picture of a very small part of the universe. It shows hundreds of galaxies, each one containing 100,000 million stars. Although God's universe is so very great, He is Spirit, and His love for us is even greater. (note on 1.2b, p. 8) this reason many scholars think that it was composed for a religious festival. Worshippers joined in repeating a chorus. See 'God said' (repeated ten times), and the three phrases which each occur six times: 'And it was so', 'God saw that it was good', 'There was evening and there was morning'.

As we would expect in a hymn of praise, the main teaching in this chapter is teaching *about God* as He makes a relationship with His creation (His name occurs thirty-four times).

1. God is the *one and only* creator of the universe, and the one cause of life within it (see notes on Gen. 1.1a, 31).

2. God is *different* from the natural world, yet its life comes from His life (see note on 1.2b).

3. God continually *sustains* what he has created (see note (c) on 1.1a and note on 1.26b).

4. God is *spirit*, and is not limited by space or time (see note on 1.2b).

5. God is *personal*, but is neither male nor female (see note on 1.5b).

6. God has *limited* His own powers by creating the universe and by giving free will and responsibility to His creation (see notes on 1.26b and 26c).

NOTES

1.1a. In the beginning God created the heavens and the earth: i.e., nothing existed before God created something. With these words, the writers, the theologians, were *interpreting* the existence of the universe. This was their 'task'. Here, as in most parts of the Bible, readers gain most from a passage if they find in it an answer to three questions:

1. What happened? (In this case the answer is, 'The universe began'.)

2. How did the writers interpret that event? As we saw above, their interpretation was, 'God created it'.

3. What is our response? As readers, we have to provide the answer.

In some English Bible versions, we read, 'When God began to create the heavens and the earth, the earth was without form' (see RSV margin). But readers using this translation might think (wrongly) that God found a universe which already existed and gave it order.

Created: The theologians who gave us this chapter used the word 'create' (Hebrew: *bara*) to mean much more than 'make'. It means:

1. *To begin a long process.* Scientists tell us that the universe began with a 'Big Bang' (see p. 20). But God's creation was not a single action. There have been many changes in it. God used and uses many

7

processes. God is still the Creator today. As we read this chapter we are reading about 'a process'. One 'day' follows another. When scientists talk about the theory of 'evolution' they are talking about a 'process' or number of 'changes'. Thus 'God creating' means that He allows what has been created to develop and to 'make itself' (see note on 1.31).

2. *To sustain and support the created universe.* God did not make the universe and then retire, leaving it to survive as well as it could without Him. He is not a spectator, just observing what happens. See note on 2.2.

3. *To create with a purpose.* The universe did *not* appear by 'blind chance'.

1.2a. The earth was without form: i.e., it was in total disorder. God gave to His universe freedom from disorder. So there is order in the universe. Many things happen regularly. Other things do happen in a 'random' or irregular way and by chance. But 'God holds all things together' (Col. 1.17b, 20). See note 2 on 1.31.

1.2b. The spirit of God was moving over the face of the waters: Spirit: The Hebrew word translated 'spirit' is *ruach* which is feminine in gender. It can mean breath or wind, but usually it is a sign of the life which God gives. God is not only 'greater than' His creation; He is *in* it. See Psalm 104.29–30.

Moving (or 'hovering' REB): i.e. like a mother-bird hovering or fluttering over her young as she feeds them. The mother-bird is not far from her young. So God is not far from us or apart from us. Since He created us He has always been with us and among us. (The Jews who wrote down this verse perhaps did not understand how important it was. But Christians should understand it. See 1 John 4.12: 'God lives *in* us'.) God is 'moving' by continually sustaining and supporting His creation.

The waters: The Hebrews were not a seafaring people and were afraid of water. In the Old Testament, when writers wrote about water they were usually thinking of its danger. See Ps. 107.23–8.

1.3. God said 'Let there be light': The Hebrew word for God's 'saying' or 'speaking is *dabar* and it has two meanings.

1. God's 'speaking' results in God's *doing* something. God said 'Let there be light', and there *was* light. See Isa. 55.11 and John 1.14, where we read that God's 'word' became flesh; the word became Jesus Christ.

2. God wants His will to become clear to us. He takes action so that we may know His will. He does not wait for us to discover it by ouselves.

1.5a. God called the light Day, and the darkness he called Night: The writers refer to God creating light here and do not write about the sun until 1.14–18. Some readers are troubled by this, saying 'Our light comes from the sun, so surely the sun was created *before* light.' But scientists tell us that light and heat existed long before our sun existed.

He:

1. This word is used here and throughout English translations of the Bible when referring to God. As a result, many people have thought that God is more masculine than feminine. Although we must use some pronoun in English, 'He' can be misleading, because God is neither masculine nor feminine. Some Chinese Christians make this plain by having a special pronoun for God. Their pronouns are:

| he | she | God | it (animal) | it (thing) |

2. But in English and many other languages the word 'He' reminds us that God is *personal*. He is not a thing ('it'), i.e. He makes relationships with His people. We can pray to Him and He hears our prayers.

Called: In the Bible 'calling' or giving something or someone a name is important:

(a) People are 'called' or 'named' for a *purpose*. See 1 Cor. 1.1.

(b) The people who call make a *relationship* with those who are called. See 2.19–20.

1.5b. The evening and the morning were the first day: Most scholars interpret the word 'day' as a stage in creation, not as a special length of time. Those who regard Gen. 1 as a *history* interpret 'day' either as 'twenty-four hours' or as a somewhat longer (but limited) period. But because Gen. 1 is like a hymn or poem, *not* a history, that interpretation should not be accepted.

1.11. Let the earth put forth vegetation, plants . . . each according to its kind: (See note on v.5b.)

Earth: When Gen. 1 was written many people thought that the earth was a sort of goddess who had to be worshipped with sacrifices. Some people today who speak of 'Mother Earth' hold a similar view. But the earth is not to be worshipped. God created it, and re-creates it and keeps it alive. We worship God Himself, not the earth.

Each according to its kind: i.e. God made a great many different sorts or 'species' of plants etc.

Plants: We read in 1. 11 and 12 how beneficial plants and trees are. Today we know much more clearly why they are beneficial and how greatly we depend on them; e.g. they provide food and shelter; trees absorb carbon dioxide from the air and turn it into the oxygen which we need in order to breathe. Many thousands of life-giving medicines come from plants and trees.

The writers who composed Genesis say here that God created plants before He created the sun. We now know that plants, such as those we see and use, cannot live without the sun's light (see note on 1.5a). But no one knew that at the time when this was written. And we should note that the aim of those writers was to praise God, not to produce a history or text-book of science.

1.16. God made the two great lights . . . he made the stars also: Just as many people regarded the earth as a goddess, so they also worshipped the sun and the moon. People still do this, even though human beings have already walked on the moon. That is the reason why the sun and moon have not been given names here. They are only called 'lights'.

In the same way people have treated the stars as if they were like gods. They have often looked for guidance from stars rather than from God. See Deut. 4.19: 'When you see the sun and the moon and the stars, do not . . . worship them.' This verse is a warning against treating anything or anyone as if they were God.

Lights . . . stars: Scientists have discovered a great deal about our sun and moon. They now know, for example, that the moon only reflects the sun's light: it does not itself give light. Today we know far more about the stars and other parts of the universe than was known in past ages. But we urgently need God's guidance in order to use the knowledge rightly. Scientists may *know* how to send a space-ship to Mars. Is it God's will that they spend billions of dollars in doing so, while millions of people are starving on earth?

1.21. God created the great sea-monsters: The word 'created' (*bara*) only occurs here, in 1.1 and 1.27. The word 'made' (Hebrew *asah*) is used elsewhere in this chapter. The writers used this word *bara* in order to emphasize God's uniqueness and authority over the whole of creation. The Babylonians taught that the sea-monsters existed *before* the creation. So the message of this verse was 'Even the sea-monsters were created by God, and are answerable to Him. There is only *one* God. Worship and trust Him!'

Questions on 1.1–25

Words:

1. What were the Hebrews saying about God when they spoke of His *ruach* (translated 'spirit') in 1.2?

Content:

2. What was the chief aim of those who wrote Gen. 1?

3. Several important truths about God appear on p. 7. Which *two* of them do you think are the most important for us today?

4. 'This passage is more like a hymn or poem than a history' (p. 5).

(a) Why does this seem to be true?

(b) Give one of the sentences in the passage which is repeated like a chorus.

Bible:

5. Which verses in Psalms 8, 104 and 136.1–9 best express the main thought of Gen. 1?

6. In what way is the teaching of each of the following like the teaching of Gen. 1? (a) Ps. 51.10 (b) John 5.17 (c) Rev. 21.5

Application:

7. (a) Tell the story of the creation of the world best known to you from traditional folk-lore;

(b) What is the chief difference between that traditional account and the account in Gen. 1?

8. 'God is neither masculine nor feminine' (p. 9). How can we show that this is true while we still call God 'Him'?

9. A student read in Gen. 1.11 and 12 that plants were created before the sun, and said, 'But plants cannot live without the sun's light. How can I take the Bible seriously?' What could you reply to him?

10. 'People have treated stars as if they were gods' (p. 10).

(a) How much do people whom you know trust the stars to give them advice or information?

(b) What can you say to those who rely on the stars for guidance?

1.26a. Let us make man: The word 'man' (Hebrew *adam*) here means 'human beings' not a male Hebrew individual. The writers do not use 'Adam' as a name until Gen. 3. In most parts of the Old Testament the writers were thinking chiefly of their own nation, the Hebrews. But in this chapter they were referring to *all* human beings. All races and nations therefore belong together. All belong to the one great 'human family', which God created. This truth was expressed by a Chinese boatman who helped a foreign professor to escape from China. The Communists had just obtained power and had declared that foreigners were 'enemies of the people'. The professor knew that the boatman was in great danger, and asked him why he had helped him. The boatman said, 'I also am a man.' This is the truth which 'racists' and 'extreme nationalists' deny. But we shall not all live together in peace unless we accept it.

According to this chapter, God made human beings to be *part* of His natural creation. The name 'Adam' comes from a Hebrew word meaning 'red earth'. Humans belong to the rest of nature; e.g. they have to get food as other creatures do. The Hebrews had no special word for 'nature', they saw *all* God's living creatures as filled with God's *nephesh* ('life'). See Prov. 12.10. (In Gen. 2 human beings are seen as the *centre* of God's natural creation, but in this chapter they are shown to be *part* of it.) The discoveries made by scientists enable us to understand this truth more fully. They say that all matter (including human bodies) comes from the same elements such as hydrogen and helium which appeared as a result of the 'Big Bang' and from other elements such as carbon and oxygen. They also show us that humans, as well as the rest of the natural world, have the same arrangement of 'molecules' in our bodies (a molecule is a very small particle, which is made up of even smaller particles called 'atoms'). And there are very many more ways in which human beings share life with the rest of the natural world, especially with animals. This truth, that we humans are part of nature, is important for all of us today. When we harm or misuse nature without restoring it, we are harming ourselves. See also notes on 1.26c, and 3.19b.

But, as is clear from 1.26b, human beings are *different from* the rest of nature. See Ps 8.4–8. We can relate to God and respond and pray to Him personally.

1.26b. In our image: The message that God made human beings 'in His image' shows us something about *His purpose* in the world:

1. To give Himself to the world because it is His nature to love and to give. See 'God so loved that He *gave* . . .' (John 3.16).

2. To share His power with us. By doing this He limited His own powers. See note on 1.26c.

3. To make a relationship with us and to seek a response.

We could say that God, because of this purpose, printed His image (His likeness) on human beings and put His life into our lives. See Eph. 3.20b, 'His power is at work within us'.

The words also contain important truth *about ourselves*:

1. God has made us to be His representatives in the world, to do what He wants to be done, to value what He most values, and to fight against the evils which He is fighting.

2. God has made *all* human beings, both men and women, in His image, therefore all human beings belong to the same family.

3. But we are not God! (see notes on 2.9, 2.17 and 3.5) We are rebellious representatives who need continual renewal.

4. Although we have spoiled and disfigured the image by our sinfulness, God has not destroyed that image. He has not abolished our relationship with Him (see Hos. 11.8, 9).

Us . . . our: By using these words instead of 'me' and 'my', the writers were perhaps comparing God to a king with His court or were thinking of God along with His angels. But there is only *one* God. Some people have imagined that the writer was here referring to the Trinity, Father, Son and Holy Spirit. But this is not so. The writers were not thinking of Jesus or the Holy Spirit as they wrote this.

1.26c. Let them have dominion: The Hebrew words translated here and in 1.28 as 'have dominion over' mean 'to be stewards, guardians, caretakers' who are answerable to God for the way in which they use His world. See also 2.15: 'care for the earth', 'guard it'. The Muslim Scripture, the Qur'an, contains a reference to this and the word *khalifa* is used, which means 'to be a deputy who is answerable to the supreme ruler'. We can see important teaching in these words:

1. God has limited His own power by letting human beings have 'dominion'. There is no limit to God's love, but His power is not 'almighty'. He willingly gives away some of it. The saying 'God can do anything He pleases' is not true. (See note 2 on God's purpose, under 1.26b (p. 12)).

2. God supports and encourages us when He gives us 'dominion'. He intends us to have some control over our surroundings. See Ps. 8.6–8.

3. But God has given 'dominion' to those whom He made 'in His image', so of course He intends them to use that dominion *responsibly*, as He does.

To give two examples: when we cut down a tree, we need to plant another (or two more) in its place so that the land does not become a desert; when we catch a fish, we need to limit the size of our catch so that enough fish remain to breed in the future. God means us to use the whole earth, its animals, plants, fish, air, soil and water, as a good

'To have dominion means to be answerable to God for the way in which we use His world' (p. 13). But in order to make quick profits we humans have destroyed two-thirds of the rain forests in the world, including this forest in Brazil, which have taken thousands of years to grow.

housewife treats her house and garden. She keeps them in good repair and ready for the next generation. She makes a relationship with the rest of God's creation. She does not just use it.

4. God thus intends us to be seriously concerned about material things such as the earth as well as for spiritual things. See note on 3.17.

Note on the misuse of 'dominion': Although human beings depend on the earth and future generations will depend upon it, they are misusing it very dangerously at present. To give three examples:

• Very many of our medicines come from the tropical rainforests which have taken thousands of years to develop. But two-thirds of those forests have already been cut down and cannot grow again, to be what they were, for hundreds of years.

• There is a limited amount in the earth of fuels such as coal, oil and gas, which give power to machines. But many nations are using them as if there was no limit.

• More and more nations are using factories to make goods and so to increase their standard of living. But the use of factories makes many people unemployed. And most factories pour out carbon dioxide gas into the air. As a result, the ice in the Arctic and Antarctic is melting and this will more and more cause flooding in low-lying countries, unless people use factories more 'responsibly'.

Why are we misusing God's earth? Partly because we have mistakenly thought that God, in giving us 'dominion', was giving us permission to waste or to destroy anything we pleased. Partly because of our sinfulness and greed, and our wish to make a quick profit. Partly because of our ignorance. Partly because we have forgotten that we show our love for God by being responsible stewards of His creation, and that we and the rest of His creation belong together. In order to survive, human beings *have to* treat the universe as something belonging to God (Ps. 24.1).

1.27. Male and female He created them: God has made men and women different physically, but according to 1. 26 and 27 He made both of them 'in His image'. And he entrusted *both* of them to care for the earth. Four times in this chapter we read that one part of the created world is separate from another part (see 1. 4b, 7a, 14, 18). But men and women are *not* separated in that way. They are partners.

Why do so many men treat women as inferior, instead of treating them as partners? There are many reasons. Men are physically stronger, and like to have power over women. Some say that according to 2.22 the first woman came from part of the man and that therefore women are inferior. Others have picked out some verses from Paul's writings, like Eph. 5.23 ('the husband is the head of the wife') and have neglected verses like 1 Cor. 7.3 ('the husband should give to his wife conjugal rights, and likewise the wife to her husband'). See also notes on 2.22; 3.20; 16.3; 29.19.

What can be done so that women are treated as 'partners'? In each generation and in each place Christians, men and women, need to answer with God's guidance, such questions as the following:

• Why should wives not share fully in the taking of decisions concerning the family?
• Why should women not receive as much education as men?
• Why are they overlooked when leaders are appointed in the Church? See also note 4 on 1.28, p. 17.

1.28. God blessed them and said, 'Be fruitful and multiply': So God gave his blessing and approval to the sexual instinct and intercourse which enables parents to be 'fruitful'. In many parts of the Old Testament there are warnings against the Canaanites and their 'high places' where they treated fertility as a god, and they saw the human sex act as a way of worshipping that god, and gaining his favour. They believed that it would help to make their crops fertile (Hos. 4.13, 14). But sex is God's gift, it is not an alternative god. However, He intends us to 'be fruitful' *responsibly.*

Multiply: When Genesis was being written, nations were behaving 'responsibly' if they 'multiplied' or they *increased* their population. They had to do this in order to survive in the face of wars and disease. But today nations will not survive unless they *control* the size of the population. If they do not, there will not be enough food and water for everyone. If that happens, there will be famine, and nations will go to war to obtain food and water.

Some governments have already passed laws to limit the number of children in a family. But all nations need to solve this problem, e.g.:

1. They can discover the facts about the increasing number of people in the world, e.g. in 1960 there were 3,000 million, in 1975 4,000, in 1995 6,000. By 2025 there may be 9,000 million (but there is not enough food for that number).

2. They can take action to ensure that the world's food is shared fairly. Grain is used unfairly at present. Each person in North America is at present using 800 kgs every year; each person in India uses only 200 kgs.

3. If the richer countries can share with the poorer countries, then the whole standard of living of the poorer countries will be improved. This will limit the population of the world for the following reason: when a family is very poor the parents feel that they need to produce a large number of children because many of them will die. In this way they hope to be supported in old age.

4. The position of women must be improved in every way. (See note on 1.27 above.)

5. Clinics must be provided where advice is given about the planning of a family. These clinics usually provide artificial birth-control (contraceptives) as well as general advice. (But Roman Catholic authorities, and many Muslims, have forbidden the use of contraceptives made by humans and have told members to use other methods of preventing unwanted babies.)

1.29. Every plant . . . you shall have them for food: Many people believe this means that we should not eat meat, either because the ways of transporting and killing the animals is very often cruel or because we and the animals belong together. See note 3 on 1.26c. But we cannot prove that eating meat is wrong from this verse. In 9.2, 3 we read 'every moving thing shall be food for you'. We make mistakes when we base our behaviour on one single verse of the Bible.

1.31. God saw that it was good: There is much evil in the world, but God's creation is itself good, not evil.

1. But many Christians have disregarded these words, and have said that only half of God's creation was good, the other half being evil, and that matter was evil.

As a result of such teaching many people have thought:

(a) that people's souls are important, but their bodies are not;

(b) that the use of sex is concerned with matter, and so should be avoided;

(c) that we need not care about the natural world, since it is evil.

This false teaching is based on some Greek thinking and is known as 'dualism' (meaning that there are 'two grades' of God's creation). But we learn from the New Testament that the Word of God Himself took flesh (John 1.14 and 2 John 7), and that His creation is one, not two. See note on 3.1.

2. But people ask, 'If God made the world good, and if God Himself is good, why is there so much pain in the world?' 'Why do thousands of innocent people die every year when there is famine or war?' Probably no one will ever be able to answer those questions, but we may note two answers which some theologians give:

(a) Most suffering is probably the result of ignorance, or the misuse of free will;

(b) Although God's creation is good, He allowed it to develop and to 'make itself'. It does not behave like a machine. We can predict some events, but God allows other events to happen at 'random'. (See note on 1.2a.)

2.2. On the seventh day God finished the work . . . and He rested:

Seventh Day: As we have seen (p. 5), this part of Genesis (1.1—2.4) was probably composed by priestly theologians in Babylon. Their task was to help the Hebrews in exile to keep the traditions of their religion. The two customs which made the Hebrews different from the others were resting on the seventh day ('Sabbath') and circumcision. So for them this verse meant that God instituted the Sabbath, the day of rest, renewal and worship.

After Jesus had risen, Christians celebrated the event by making the 'first day' their special day. See Acts 20.7. This day, now called Sunday, is a day for rest, refreshment and worship, and for members of a family to enjoy each other. And we urgently need to use it in those ways.

Rested: So the first stages of God's work of creating were complete and He rested for 'a day'. But God did not retire when He had made men and women in His image (1.27). He has always been the sustainer and re-creator of all His creation (see Acts 17.28). He is the life-force in all that lives.

Questions on 1.26—2.4a

Words:

1. (a) What does the Hebrew word *adam* mean?
   (b) What does it refer to in this chapter?

Content:

2. (a) God made human beings to be part of nature (p. 12).
   (b) Human beings are different from the rest of nature (p. 12).
   Comment on each of those statements and explain why it makes a difference to our lives if we believe it.

3. 'Let us make man in our image' (1.26a). What do we learn about God from those words?

4. 'Let them have dominion' (1.26c).
   (a) Give an example of someone using that 'dominion' responsibly.
   (b) Why are many people misusing it?

5. 'Men and women are partners' (p. 15). Why do many men not treat their wives in that way?

6. What is the difference between the Jewish Sabbath and the Christian Sunday?

Bible:

7. What relationship between husband and wife do each of the

18

following verses describe? (a) 1 Cor. 7.3 (b) 1 Cor. 11.3 (c) Eph. 5.22, 23 (d) 1 Pet. 3.7. Do the writers contradict each other?

Application:

8. 'Have dominion' (1.26c). Give two examples of people *mis*using the earth.

9. 'Nations will not survive unless they control the size of their population (p. 16).
  (a) What is your opinion?
  (b) If populations must be limited, what are the right ways?

10. If God made the world good, why is there so much pain (p. 17)? What is your opinion of the two answers given on that page?

Special Note A:
Theologians and Scientists

Theologians and scientists need each other. Each group has its own special task, its own way of learning about and interpreting the universe. Both groups aim to tell the truth, but they talk about different things. We might compare this to asking a man to tell us about his wife. He might say that she is aged 40 and weighs 55 kgs. Or that he loves her dearly and believes that she loves him. The two statements could *both* be true. Theologians and scientists are partners: both use the intelligence which God has given them. Both base their beliefs on experience and evidence. Both aim to discover more: both understand that there is much that they do not yet know. Both see the universe with awe and wonder. The great scientist Einstein said that he saw it 'with rapturous amazement'.

Scientists are making new discoveries all the time, so that their opinions change, but their special tasks remain:

1. To gain knowledge by observing things which they can weigh or measure. God cannot be measured in that way, so scientists cannot prove either that He does or does not exist.

2. To ask and answer questions concerning the universe such as 'What?', 'How?' and 'When?' (Theologians, on the other hand, try to answer the question 'Why?' – 'What was God's purpose?')

So the scientists' task is to ask and answer such questions as:

(a) *What exists today?* Their answer: The earth we live on is one of nine planets which move round the sun. The sun is one of about 100,000 million stars in our 'galaxy' or group of stars to which the earth belongs. There are more than 100,000 million galaxies in the universe.

(b) *How did it begin?* Most scientists answer: The universe arose from a single 'instant' or 'point' (which is too small for most people to imagine) in an enormous explosion which scientists call the 'Big Bang'. In that one 'instant' space and time and matter and energy began to exist. As space expanded and cooled, fragments of matter and energy combined together and formed galaxies of stars. These galaxies still continue to rush away from each other.

(c) *When did the universe begin?* Most scientists answer: It began about 15,000 million years ago. The earth is about 4,600 million years old. Life first appeared on earth about 4,000 million years ago. Creatures with hard skeletons appeared about 700 million years ago, mammals about 180 million years ago. The first human beings of an undeveloped sort appeared about 400,000 years ago, and the more developed humans came into being less than 100,000 years ago.

Those are the answers which most scientists are giving at the present time. How do people respond to those ideas? We note here various ways in which they respond:

1. Most Christians and others who try to understand what the scientists are saying are filled with wonder at the size and age of God's universe. Concerning its *size* they know that, according to scientists, the universe is far bigger than people once thought. Some Christians ask, 'If this is so, how can God care for me?' But God is Spirit (John 4.24). He is present everywhere. His love is not in any way affected by the size of His universe.

Concerning the age of the universe, most scientists say that nothing existed before the 'Big Bang'. There was no time, and so there was no 'before'! Some ask, 'If this is so, how could God have been there to create the universe?' But God is not a 'thing'. Also, He was never separated from our world (see note on 1.2b).

2. But some Christians, who are usually called '*biblical creationists*', do not agree with the scientists' ideas. They say, for example:

(i) that God dictated each word of Gen. 1, and He did not simply give life and encouragement to those who were trying to understand His universe;

(ii) that in Gen. 1 we have the true and accurate history of the creation, and that it is not a hymn or poem;

(iii) that God has never changed what He once created, and that things are today exactly what they were at the beginning. 'Evolution' has not taken place.

3. Some scientists (who agree with the information given on p. 20) believe that God cannot exist. One reason they give is that nothing can exist except what scientists can observe. Others say that the universe was caused by 'blind chance'. Others say it is 'simply a machine'.

Many Christians have been deeply troubled by the statements of such scientists. But we should note that not all 'scientists' hold the same opinions. Some believe in God and some do not.

Questions on Special Note A

1. Describe one thing which theologians and scientists can both do.

2. Why are scientists not able to prove either that God does or does not exist?

3. What is a 'galaxy'?

4. Seeing that the world is so much older and larger than people once thought, how could God care about each of us?

5. Some Christians say that evolution never happened and that God has never allowed things to change which He created.
  (a) Why do they say that?
  (b) What is your opinion?

2.4b–25
Humanity's Opportunity

OUTLINE

2.4b–6: God fertilizes a dry desert with water.

2.7: From the moist clay He makes a man, and gives him life.

2.8–9: God makes a garden and plants trees.

2.10–14: A note about the rivers flowing from the garden.

2.15: God gives the man the task of caring for the garden.

2.16–17: God shows the man which trees to use and which trees he must not use.

2.18–22: God provides animals among whom the man will live, and finally He makes a woman to be the man's wife.

2.23: The man rejoices that he has a wife.

2.24: A note about the man's loyalty to his wife.

2.25: The man and the woman enjoy each other sexually.

INTERPRETATION

These are some of the questions which readers often ask about these verses:

1. *Why is there a second account of creation?* It may seem to be a second account but it is not really a repetition of Gen. 1. Gen. 1 is a

hymn or poem about God creating the whole universe, but Gen. 2 is mainly about God making human beings. And there are other differences:

(a) In this chapter they use a different name for God. See note on 2.4b.

(b) Here they say that God 'made' the world, but in Gen. 1 God 'created' it.

(c) As we read Gen. 1 we feel that God is majestic. Although He created humans in His image (1.26a), yet He is distinct from them. But in Gen. 2 and 3 God is more like humans. See 2.3 and 3.8.

(d) The order of events is different. In Gen. 1 God makes human beings at the end of creation; in Gen. 2 He makes the man *before* the plants and animals.

2. *Who wrote Gen. 2?* Most scholars believe that its stories were collected together in about 900 BC (that is about 500 years before Gen. 1 was compiled), and that editors put the two chapters together in about 400 BC. See Special Note B, p. 40.

3. *Is Gen. 2 a history of the first human beings or a parable about all humans?* The writers of Gen. 2, like most of the people who wrote the Bible, were in the habit of using *parables*, symbols and poetry in order to express the greatest truths. See 2.7 where 'breathed' is a symbol of God giving life to humans. Jesus spoke in this way, e.g. when He called Himself a good 'shepherd'. Certainly we discover far more of the message of Gen. 2 if we regard it as a parable, and this is how we interpret it in this commentary.

4. *What is the message of Gen. 2 for us?* The message is about *opportunity* and *warning*.

(a) God in His fatherly care has given human beings the *opportunity* to live a good life in relationship with Him. He has provided them with what they need. We notice the gifts which God gave them: life (2.7), food (2.8, 9), work (2.15), freedom to choose between right and wrong (2.16, 17), fellowship with others (2.18, 21–4), sexuality (2.25).

(b) But we human beings are being *warned* that we cannot enjoy these opportunities unless we trust God humbly as the creator on whom we depend. We are His creatures. He is in charge of the world and we are only His tenants (see notes on 2.17).

NOTES

2.4b. The Lord God made the earth and the heavens: The name for God in Hebrew manuscripts of Gen. 1 is *Elohim*. But here in Gen. 2 it is *Yahweh Elohim*. In some verses of Gen. 3 it is *Yahweh* (which early translators wrongly translated 'Jehovah').

2.7a. The Lord God formed man of dust of the ground:

Man: The making of human beings is the chief subject of this chapter. As soon as moisture existed God formed a human being, as a potter makes a figure out of clay.

Dust: We are made out of earthy material, like dust, which is temporary. See 3.19. Thus we are creatures dependent on God.

Ground: The Hebrew word for 'ground' is *adamah* and the word for 'man' is *adam*. The writer was in this way showing the link between them. We humans belong to the ground. We live well when we co-operate with the natural world.

But we are more than 'dust of the ground'. God has given us the opportunity to relate to Him. See 1 Cor. 15.47–50. As St Augustine said, 'You have made us for Yourself, and our hearts are restless till they rest in You.'

2.7b. And breathed into his nostrils the breath of life: By doing this God was not simply giving the man breath. He was giving His spirit, His own life, Himself. See Ezek. 37.1–6 and John 3.16: 'God so loved . . . that He gave . . .'. Human beings are thus dependent on God. They are creatures, they are not God!

2.7c. Man became a living being: The Hebrew word *nephesh* translated here in most modern versions as 'living being' means 'person' or 'self'. In the AV it was translated 'soul', which could mislead us. 'Soul' sounds as if God gave the man a separate thing called 'soul' to add to his body. But God made us unified beings. We do not have totally separate parts called bodies and minds and souls. We *are* body, we *are* mind and we *are* soul. So those whose work is to heal others need to consider the *whole* of the person who is in need. See note on 1.31.

2.8. God planted a garden in Eden . . . and there put the man: Many people have thought that 'Eden' means a place for perfect human beings, and that we should do our best to go back to that life. But we do not find that teaching stated in this chapter. Certainly, according to Gen. 2 Adam was neither cruel nor selfish. But neither do we read that he was kind or honest.

Eden is a symbol or picture-language for human beings who are untested, incomplete and immature. 'Eden' is thus an opportunity which God offers to humanity. As we saw, *adam* means 'human beings'. Each of us began as immature, and God intends us to grow up, with His grace, 'until we attain to maturity' (Eph. 4.13).

Note: Long after Genesis was written, Greeks called the garden of Eden 'paradise' from a Persian word meaning a 'pleasure ground'. They also used this word for life after death (see Luke 23.43).

2.9. The tree of life . . . the tree of the knowledge of good and evil: This is the first of many statements about *trees* in Gen. 2 and 3. Some readers are confused because these statements do not always agree; for example in 2.17 and 3.3 God gives them the gift of living for ever, and warns them not to lose it, but in 3.22b God is preventing them from living for ever.

Perhaps the reason for such 'disagreements' is that the editors were combining two different traditions. But, whatever the reason, the stories about trees point readers to extremely important truths for all human beings, especially about our sinful wish to be equal to God and independent of Him. (See notes on 2.17, 3.3, 3.5, 3.22, 3.24.)

Tree of life: This tree only occurs here and in 3.22. Its meaning is: 'Anyone who eats from this tree will "live for ever" '.

Tree of knowledge of good and evil: This tree is a symbol of the knowledge which only God possesses. Eating from this tree means thinking that we are 'like' God Himself and know as much as He knows about good and evil (see note on 2.17).

2.10. A river flowed out of Eden: In these notes we have interpreted 'Eden' as a symbol or picture language (see note on 2.8). But in 2. 10–14 the writers have regarded it as a place, situated in the country now called Iraq, from which four rivers flowed. Tigris and Euphrates are there today.

Questions on 2.4b–14

Words:

1. 'Man became a living being' (2.7b).

(a) What is the meaning of the word which is here translated 'living being'?

(b) How accurate is the translation given in another English version or another language which you know?

Content:

2. (a) Name two differences between this account of creation and the account in Gen. 1.

(b) Why are they different?

3. (a) What two sorts of trees are described here?

(b) Eating the fruit of one of those trees was a symbol of a human sin. What sin?

4. 'God breathed' (2.7). Give another example of symbolism or 'picture language' which the writers used in Gen. 2 to refer to God's activity.

Bible:

5. The note on p. 24 shows that human beings are (a) 'dust of the ground' and (b) more than dust. Which of the following passages

---

point to (a), and which point to (b)? Gen. 3.19; Job 10.9; Ps. 8.5; Ps. 104.29; John 17.2

Application:

6. There are two interpretations of the Garden of Eden on p. 24. Which do you think is the true one? Give reasons.

7. 'Our sinful wish to be equal to God and independent of Him' (p. 25). Give examples of people
    (a) trying to be independent of Him
    (b) living as creatures who are dependent on Him.

2.15. Put him in the garden to till it and keep it: His work was to develop it and to keep it in good order. God has made human beings responsible for looking after the earth. See notes on 1.26, 1.28 and 3.17–18. Here is one example of looking after the soil so that it gives the best results: farmers give it animal manure, and plant a crop, then they let the soil rest for a year and then plant a different crop. But when farmers want to get crops as quickly as possible, they may disregard this method and use strong fertilizers which kill the bees and poison the streams below.

We need to 'till and keep' the soil, not only because governments may have told us to do so, but because God has made the world in this way. Caring for the earth is being obedient to Him. It is part of our faith!

We also see from this verse that God intends us to have work to do, so that we can serve the community and keep healthy. But in some countries many people are without work, especially in big cities. In other places people, even children, are overworking to save their families from starvation. Being obedient to God means helping people to find work, and preventing the ill-treatment of children.

2.16. You may freely eat: This verse, like the whole of this chapter, describes the fatherly care of God, who provides for our needs. We see His care and love most clearly in the teaching about God which Jesus gave. See Luke 12.28.

2.17. Of the tree of the knowledge of good and evil you shall not eat, for in the day that you eat of it you shall die: Eating from this tree was sinful because it meant thinking that they knew as much as God knows about what is good and what is evil. See 3.5, where the sin is called 'being *as* God' (AV) or 'being like God himself' (REB), that is, being equal to God. This is the root human sin, and Gen. 2—11 all draw attention to it. See 11.4a, 6. When we fall into this sin we no longer live as creatures who are answerable to God. We become self-important, as if we could be independent of God, and as if we were our own

'God has made human beings responsible for looking after the earth' (p. 26).

By means of the Kariba Dam men have controlled the waters of the river Zambesi. They have created a new lake, 250 km long, between Zambia and Zimbabwe.

authority. Muslims are well aware of this sin. The Arabic word *shirk* means treating anyone or anything as if they were on a level with God. (So this sin is more serious then disobedience. Disobedient people know that there is a greater authority, although they reject it.)

Some scientists are saying that people may be able to manufacture human beings by 'cloning' (i.e. not by natural sex reproduction). Many Christians believe that, if they do this, they will be trying to be 'equal with God'.

You shall die: Perhaps the writers thought that God was afraid that human beings would live for ever, *or* that He had intended humans to be immortal, and that death was always a punishment for sin. See Rom. 5.12.

But in other passages dying is a part of being a human being. In 3.22 God expected 'the man' to die. Most writers in the Bible believed the same. For example, Eccles. 3.2: 'There is a time to live and a time to die.'

2.18a. It is not good that a man should be alone: Throughout Gen. 2 we learn that God made human beings to live 'in relationship': with God Himself (2.7), with the soil (2.15), with other creatures (2.20) And in this verse we read about the relationship between men and women.

God's plan is that most people should find a partner to marry, that they should give themselves to their wife or husband and in doing so fulfil their own true nature. But many men and women live full and useful lives without marrying. Jesus never married.

But God intends everyone, whether married or unmarried, to live in relationship with other people, to support them and to be supported by them, to work with them in the local community, to belong to a Christian congregation rather than being a 'lone Christian' (see note on 12.2).

2.18b. I will make him a helper, fit for him: Once again we read about God's fatherly care for the man whom He had made. He planned to find him a 'helper'.

Some people have thought that women are inferior to men because in this passage God made the woman *after* He had made the man, and because He made her to be the man's 'helper or assistant'. But this is a totally false interpretation. The Hebrew word for 'helper' is *ezer*. In the Bible it often means a stronger person who can help a weaker person. In Ps. 33.20 God is called our *ezer*. (See also Exod. 18.4, Deut. 33.7.) Some have therefore thought that God made women superior to men. But this is not so. Men and women are equal partners. (This 'equal partnership' is much more clearly stated in Gen. 1, e.g. in 1.27, than in Gen. 2.)

2.20. The man gave names: 'Giving the creatures names' means relating to them, being responsible for them, caring for them as far as is possible, rather than mastering them, destroying them or being cruel to them. We are answerable to God for the way in which we relate to animals, who are our fellow-creatures. (But see note on 3.14.)

2.22. The rib which the Lord God had taken from the man he made into a woman: These words, like many other words in Gen. 2 and 3, are 'picture language' (symbolic). The meaning here is that women are of the same nature as men. They do not mean that women are inferior to men or of less value. (See notes on 2.18b and 3.16b.)

Some people think that St Paul, following traditional Jewish interpretation, did see women as inferior. See 1 Cor. 11.7, 8: 'Man is the glory of God, but woman is the glory of man. For man was not made from woman but woman from man.' On the other hand Paul differed from Jewish tradition in 1 Cor. 11.11 and taught that men and women 'depend on each other', i.e. they need each other equally (Gal. 3.28).

2.23. This at last is bone of my bone: Here is the man's joyful shout of gratitude as he enters on intimate union with the woman. The Hebrew words can be translated 'This at last is the moment!' So here, as in 2.25, we see that sexual union between a man and a woman is God's gift for which we can rejoice. See notes on 2.25 and 3.7. (See also the Song of Solomon.) But this is one of His gifts which we very often misuse. We are answerable to Him for the way in which we use it.

In the second part of this verse we read that 'woman was taken out of man'. The Hebrew word for 'woman' is *ishshah* and the word for 'man' is *ish*. So the writers were saying, 'Just as these words sound as if they belong together, so man and woman belong together.'

2.24. Therefore a man leaves his father and his mother and cleaves to his wife: This is a note by the writers of Genesis and should be printed in brackets. The writers were explaining why men left their parents when they got married. Such men were not being disloyal to their parents. They were entering into a new relationship or bond which was even closer than the parent-and-child relationship. When this verse was written, Jews were polygamists (see note on 16.3). So the writers were not here referring to monogamy. However, in New Testament times, the Jews were no longer polygamists, and Christians, following Jesus, used this verse to teach the close relationship between a man and his one wife. (See Matt. 19.5, Mark 10.6–9, Eph. 5.31.)

2.25. They were not ashamed: As in 2.23 we read here of the joy of sexual union between a man and his wife, one of God's gifts. But since this is God's gift, why have some Christians seen sexual intercourse as shameful? Why have they regarded unmarried people as superior to married ones? (See note on 3.7.)

Questions on 2.15–25

Words:

1. What is the Hebrew word translated 'helper' in 2.18b? What does it mean? Why is it important to know its meaning?

Content:

2. What example is given on p. 26 of someone looking after the soil 'responsibly'?

3. In the note on 2.17 five phrases are used to refer to the basic human sin.

(a) Which of these phrases do you think is the most suitable to use if you are trying to convince someone that sin is serious?

(b) Can you suggest a better phrase?

4. What does 'giving names' mean in 2.20?

Bible:

5. 'Perhaps the writers thought that death is always a punishment for sin' (p. 28). In which three of the following verses do we find that thought? Ps. 23.4; Eccles. 3.2; Wisd. 2.23–4; Matt. 23.34; Rom. 5.12; 1 Cor. 15.21

6. Read 2.24. (a) What teaching was Jesus giving when He quoted this verse in Mark 10.2–9?

(b) What teaching was Paul giving in Eph. 5.31?

Application:

7. According to 2.15 God gave 'man' work to do. But very many people today have no work they can do for their community.

(a) What is the reason?

(b) How can those who are 'unemployed' be helped?

3.1–24
Humanity's Sin and Suffering

Outline

3.1–5: The temptation to be independent of God.
3.6–7: The man and woman give in to the temptation.
3.8–13: God sternly questions them and they respond.
3.14–19: The painful result of their sinfulness.

3.20–1: God is their saviour as well as their judge.
3.22–4: But they lose their opportunity to have complete fellowship with God.

INTERPRETATION

This chapter is often called the 'story of the Fall', and has been interpreted by Christians in different ways. For example:

1. Two people, who lived a very long time ago and who were perfect, committed one sinful action and so 'fell' from perfection. Some people add that these two people corrupted all human nature, and that we have all inherited their sinfulness through our parents.

2. This chapter is about the sinfulness of all human beings. We all 'fall' from the sort of life which God means us to live. (We do not need to know at what *time* humans began to sin.)

In the notes below we follow the second of these interpretations. If we regarded Gen. 3 as an account of two individuals, we should probably miss the teaching about ourselves which we urgently need (see note on 3.6). We read in Gen. 2 of the *opportunities* which God offered to us human beings. In Gen. 3 we see our *failure* to accept these opportunities, the failure which is 'sin'.

This teaching is:

1. That we human beings, in using our God-given freewill, continually refuse to accept His authority and try to be independent of Him.

2. This sinfulness results in suffering, especially the pain of being separated from those with whom we need to live in harmony.

3. But God does not stop caring about us (see notes on 3.9, 21, 24).

NOTES

3.1 The serpent ... said to the woman: This serpent represents temptation, the temptation to make evil decisions. We note:

(a) The serpent seems in this verse to come from outside the woman, but most temptation comes from within us.

(b) The man and the woman do no wrong by being tempted. They only sin when they give in to the temptation.

(c) The writers were not here writing about 'Satan' or 'the Devil'. No Old Testament writer says that the serpent was 'Satan'. They did not refer to Satan at all until much later, e.g. in 1 Chron. 21.1. After that time Jews did call temptation 'Satan' and Mark used the name of Satan when saying that Jesus was tempted (Mark 1.13). But whatever words are used we know that temptation is strong and that we need help in resisting it.

We know also that there is only one God. We saw in the note on 1.31 (p. 17), that some Christians split God's creation into two parts, seeing one part as good, the other as evil (the false teaching called 'dualism'). Some interpret this chapter in the same way, as if there were two gods, one good and one evil. But God *made* the serpent (3.1). It was not an alternative god: it is not an alternative god now. God is in charge. This verse is not an explanation of why evil exists. We do not know why there is evil.

3.2. Did God say 'You shall not eat of any tree': i.e. 'Are you sure that God really said that?' The serpent does not openly tell the woman to be disloyal to God. It is 'subtle' (3.1) and far more dangerous than it appears to be. It cleverly twists the truth (see 3.3–5), and suggests to the woman that she is free to have her own opinion about God's plans. Our own temptations often feel like a reasonable argument. They look far less dangerous than they really are.

3.3. You shall not eat of the fruit . . . lest you die: This seems to mean that they would live for ever on this earth if they did not eat the fruit. But see notes on 2.17 and 3.19b.

3.5. God knows that when you eat of it . . . you will be like God: Other translations say 'Be like God Himself'. AV has 'be *as* God', that is to say, be on a level with God, living as if there were no authority except yourselves. See note on 2.17. One example of behaving like this is when scientists are doing experiments and saying, 'Whatever we are able to do is *right* to do.' In saying that they are behaving 'as God'. In 1945 a group of scientists discovered that they were able to make an atomic bomb. One of the group said, 'Yes, we are able to make it, but it would be wrong.' The others did not agree. The result is that nations live more in fear of each other than ever before.

The serpent seems to be saying that God is afraid that you will take away His authority, as if God were like teachers who are afraid that their pupils may know as much as they themselves do. But God is not envious. In Exod. 20.5, He is called 'jealous', but this does not mean 'envious'. It means 'zealous' or 'eager' to give the best sort of life to His people. God has created us so that we may use the intelligence He has given us ('love Him with all your mind', Mark 12.33) and to obtain all the information we can about His world. We do not sin when we use our curiosity and do research, and gain new knowledge. But we do go wrong when we use our information as if we were God, and as if there were no higher authority than ourselves.

3.6. She took of its fruit and she ate, and she also gave some to her husband and he ate: She took: i.e. she committed the sin against

'Living as if there were no authority except yourselves' (p. 32).

The Captain of this oil tanker had maps to show which route a large ship must take to avoid rocks and sandbanks in the English Channel. But on a voyage to Wales he disregarded the maps, and took a 'short cut' which he thought would be better. The result was very serious: the ship ran aground and was wrecked. Not only was the whole of its cargo of oil wasted, but as a result of the oil in the sea, thousands of fish and birds died, and parts of the sea coast ceased to produce vegetation.

which the warning was given (2.9). But as we saw in the note on p. 31, this sin is the sin of us all. We all need to be forgiven by God, and He offers us His love and support when we wish to make a fresh start (see note on 3.21).

Some of those who regard 'the woman' as one person (rather than a symbol of all humans) point to the result of her action. They say that as she bore children, her 'original' sinfulness was physically transmitted to all future generations through the process of childbirth.

And he ate: Adam was equally guilty. Many people have failed to notice this and have seen 'the woman' as the origin of sin, e.g. in the Apocrypha, in Ecclesiasticus 25.24: 'From a woman sin had its beginning, and because of her we all sin.' Because of this misinterpretation, many women are regarded as, by nature, more guilty than men, and they are prevented from being leaders in some churches.

3.7. They knew that they were naked and they sewed leaves together: i.e. they wore clothes, *either* because they were now mature adults *or* because their earlier free relationship (2.25) had been spoilt as a result of their sin.

Nakedness is not shameful or sinful; for example, we are naked when we have a bath, and doctors sometimes need to examine us naked. But many people misuse their nakedness, and film-makers and advertisers often lead others to sin by the way in which they show naked people.

But others have mistakenly thought that sexual intercourse and nakedness were themselves sinful. They have said, for example:
- that 'knowing good and evil' (3.5) means knowing about sex;
- that having sexual intercourse is sinful except for childbirth;
- that it was 'the original sin';
- that for this reason the man and woman had to cover themselves.

But writers of Genesis did not mean that. Hebrews saw sexuality as one of God's good gifts. It was often misused but it was good. Why have people followed that wrong interpretation? Partly because they thought that Paul supported it (e.g. in 1 Cor. 7.8), and partly because they were influenced by people who regarded our bodies as evil things (see 1 Tim. 4.1–3: 'they forbid marriage'). As a result many people have believed sexual sin to be more serious than other sin, and regarded unmarried people as superior to married ones. See note on 1.31.

3.8. The Lord God walking in the garden: In 3.8–13 God is putting questions to these sinful people. In 3.8 the writers describe God as very much like a human being who takes a walk in the cool evening air.

(a) God's 'walking' is a symbol of the loving care which He has for us all. He came looking for the man and the woman (3.9). Compare the shepherd in Jesus' parable of the lost sheep (Luke 15.4).

(b) God *judges* them because He loves them. Our sins damage us and if God did not point them out (as He does in 3.11–19) He would not be loving. Parents who never correct their children are careless, not caring (see Heb. 12.7–11).

3.9. Where are you?: See also 'Who?' (3.11) and 'What?' (3.13). This is one of the many passages in the Bible where God, by asking questions, shows people the truth about themselves.

3.10. I was afraid because I was naked: In 3.10–13 we see the response which the man and the woman make to God. The man has defied God's authority by taking the fruit. But, being afraid, the only fault he admits is that he is not wearing clothes.

3.12. The man said, 'The woman whom thou gavest to be with me, she gave me fruit': The man now puts the blame on the woman, and also on God (for having given him such a weak wife). And the woman blames the serpent (3.13). So we humans often find someone else to blame when we have done wrong, perhaps our parents, or the government, or God. But when we do this we are forgetting that we are free to make our own decisions.

Questions on 3.1–13

Words:
1. What is the difference between 'sin' and 'temptation'?

Contents:
2. 'Some people have mistakenly thought that sexual intercourse and nakedness were themselves sinful' (p. 34).
    (a) Why did people think that?
    (b) What is their right use?

3. God's 'walking' is a symbol (p. 34). Quote two other symbolic words in these verses.

4. What did Adam and Eve do when they heard God coming?

Bible:
5. 'Where are you?' (3.9). 'God shows people the truth about themselves by asking them questions' (p. 35). In the following passages, who heard God's question, and what truth did they learn about themselves? Gen. 4.10, 1 Kings 19.9, Job 38.4, Isa. 6.8, Ezek. 37.3, Acts 9.4

Application:
6. Two different interpretations of this chapter appear on p. 31. Which of them do you accept? Give your reasons.

---

7. 'Film-makers and advertisers often lead others to sin by the way in which they show naked people' (p. 34).
(a) How true is this in your area?
(b) How harmful is it?
8. 'We often find someone else to blame when we have done wrong' (p. 35).
(a) If you think this is true, give an example from your own experience.
(b) How can we avoid doing this?

3.14. The Lord God said to the serpent . . . 'cursed are you . . . dust you shall eat': In 3.14–18 we learn that when we sin we cause suffering for ourselves, for others, and for the world around us, for example the serpent. We saw in 3.7 that the harmony between the man and the woman was spoilt because of their defiance of God. Sinfulness results in the pain of separation.

In 3.14 the writers were asking the questions, 'Why do snakes not walk upright?' and 'Why do they bite us?', and their answer was 'Because God cursed them'. But snakes do not do right or wrong, and are not 'guilty'. 'God cursed the serpent' means that God declared that it would suffer. God has made His world one: when one part sins or suffers, other parts suffer. Paul wrote, 'The whole creation has been groaning . . . together' (Rom. 8.22). Human beings have caused suffering to reptiles and animals in many ways, and still do so.

Dust you shall eat: Snakes eat insects, worms and small animals, not dust. Some readers are troubled that the Bible here contains an error. But we do not read the Bible in order to discover the diet of reptiles.

3.16a. In pain you will bring forth your children: For many years theologians taught that because the woman in this chapter did wrong, all women must suffer in childbirth. For this reason doctors were at one time forbidden to relieve women's pain in childbirth. This was a seriously wrong interpretation. Clearly, interpreting the Bible rightly is important for many reasons.

3.16b. Your desire shall be for your husband and he shall rule over you: The writers were not saying here that men *ought* to rule over their wives, but that this was one result of the sinfulness of the first men and women. However, partly because of this verse, men claim that God wants wives to be 'subject' to them (see 1 Tim. 2.11, 12). So among many people, wives became the property of men. In the Islamic Scripture, the Qur'an, Sura 4, we read, 'Men are in charge of women, because Allah has made one of them to excel the other.'

On the other hand, according to 1.27, husbands and wives are created to be partners, as Paul says in Gal. 3.28. As a result of this teaching in many Christian marriage services the man promises to 'love and cherish' his wife. He does not claim the right to rule over her.

3.17. Cursed be the ground because of you: The meaning is 'Because of human sinfulness, the ground will become spoilt. It was spoilt by floods and earthquakes before human beings existed, and it is being spoilt in those ways today. But much spoiling is indeed 'because of' our greed or ignorance. To give two examples:

● If we cut down trees which prevent the precious top-soil from being blown or washed away, and fail to plant new ones, we are left with poor soil.

● If we use too much chemical fertilizer, the soil itself becomes poorer and poorer.

Note: Some Christians have taught that because God cursed the ground, Christians should not concern themselves with earthy or fleshly things. They should only care about their 'souls' and the 'souls' of others. But throughout the Bible obeying God means caring for and enjoying His natural earth. See notes on 1.26b, 1.31, and 2.15. See also Ps. 96.12, Ps. 104.14 and 1 John 4.2b, where we read that Jesus came into the world 'in the flesh', i.e. with a body as 'earthy' as our own.

3.18. Thorns and thistles it shall bring forth to you: Another result of their sin is that much work will be a heavy burden. Often owing to the greed or cruelty of others, much work is painful. Either it is too heavy a burden or it is dangerous, or causes illness and death, or the workers are badly paid, or forced to make useless or harmful things. But work is still God's gift, as we saw in 2.15. We co-operate with God when we make things and grow food, in spite of the 'thorns and thistles', and we have pleasure in doing so.

3.19b. Till you return to the ground: By eating from the 'tree of life' they showed that they were wanting to live for ever on this earth. See notes on 2.17 and 3.3. Indeed most people do not like to think that they will one day die. Many worry and overwork in order to forget death. See Jesus' parable in Luke 12. 16–21. God has limited our life here and we shall all die. But He has also promised believers life after death. See John 3.16; 14.2.

Some people have said that if humans had not sinned, we would all live for ever on earth. Perhaps St Paul followed this teaching in Rom. 5.12. But see notes on Gen. 2.17 and 3.22.

3.20. The man called his wife's name Eve: The Hebrew word which is here translated 'Eve' sounds like another Hebrew word which means 'living'. Some scholars interpret this verse in the following way: 'There is hope! In spite of human sinfulness God will give us life, and He will do it through a woman.'

Everyone knows that 'the woman' committed the sin of taking fruit from the tree, but we have already seen passages where a different part of her nature is seen: 1.27, where she is the equal partner of her husband, and 2.18, where she is the *ezer* or 'strong partner'. In the rest of the Bible some women are treated as important: Deborah, Ruth, Esther and, in a very special way, Mary the mother of Jesus. But as we read Genesis 12—50 we shall notice that writers nearly always show men as the important ones. Abraham, Isaac and Jacob are regarded as if they alone were the founders of the Chosen People. But we know that their mothers and their wives were equally responsible for the future generations!

3.21. God made for Adam and his wife garments of skins: We read here about God's 'grace'. He clothes them, not because they are good but because He is loving. See also note on 4.15. Paul wrote (Rom. 3.24): 'Christians are justified by His grace as a gift.'

Because God treats us in this way, He expects us to treat other people in that way. We can give help to friends who cannot repay us, or relieve the sufferings of refugees or of AIDS victims, or visit someone who is dying, or show forgiveness to a neighbour who has injured us. But we do it not because those people are good, but because we have experienced God's love.

3.22. Lest he . . . take also of the tree of life and live for ever: See note on 3.19b. The writers were saying, 'God thought that if the man stayed in the garden and ate from the tree of life, he might live for ever on this earth.'

We saw in 3.5 that eating from that tree was trying to be 'equal to God', that is, putting themselves in God's place, trying to do what only God can do. Perhaps some scientists are trying to commit that sin with their experiments. See note on 2.17 and Question 6 on p. 39.

3.24. He drove out the man . . . and placed the cherubim: God drove him out to prevent him repeating that sin. Through that sin, he had already lost the opportunity of complete fellowship with God. But God did not forget him. He was not totally lost. God took action so that we human beings could be at one with Him. His call of Abraham seems to be His first step (12.1–3). And the coming of Jesus was His great act of rescue.

Cherubim: Israelites regarded them as superhuman beings who were God's messengers. Carved figures of them were placed in places of worship. Later writers called them 'angels'.

Questions on 3.14–24

Words:

1. This chapter is about humans rejecting God's 'authority'.
   (a) What does 'authority' mean in that sentence?
   (b) Give examples of someone who does accept (i) God's authority (ii) The authority of another person.

Content:

2. 'Sinfulness results in the pain of separation' (p. 36). Give examples of this
   (a) from 3.14–19
   (b) from your own experience.

3. 'Your husband shall rule over you' (3.16b).
   (a) Why did God say that?
   (b) What reply can you give to a husband who says that those words apply to every marriage?

Bible:

4. 'God will give us life. And He will do it through a woman' (p. 37).
   (a) In the following verses,
      (i) who are the women through whom God gives new life?
      (ii) in what way did life and peace come through them?
         Gen. 21.1 and 2, 1 Sam. 1.20, Matt. 1.18, Luke 1.13.
   (b) Show how God is doing this today.

Application:

5. 'Most people do not like to think that they will one day die. Many worry and overwork in order to forget death' (p. 37).
   (a) What is your opinion?
   (b) Does believing in a life after death solve the problem?

6. 'The sin of putting themselves in God's place' (p. 38). Some doctors are putting pigs' hearts into people's bodies in order to save their lives.
   (a) What is your opinion of this sort of experiment?
   (b) Is it an example of the sin of putting ourselves in God's place, or is it rightly using the skills which God has given us?
   (c) Give an example of the sin of putting ourselves in God's place.

Special Note B:
The Writers of Genesis

In reading the Book of Genesis we have already noticed passages in which one verse does not agree with another verse, or where one passage does not agree with another passage, e.g. if we compare Gen. 1 and 2. Another example concerns people and their work. In 2.15 it is said that God intended people to work hard. But in 3.17–19 it seems that Adam has to work hard because he has sinned. These differences cause confusion to readers until it is suggested that the Book of Genesis contains the writings of more than one person. If this is so, then we say that one 'writer' gave us Gen. 1, and a different 'writer' gave us Gen. 2 and 3, and that the two were placed together at the beginning of the Book of Genesis.

Scholars suggest that the Book of Genesis had three 'writers':

1. The 'writer' of Gen. 1.1—2.4a, who also wrote other parts of Genesis. People think that he lived 600 or perhaps 500 years before Christ. As he was probably a priest, people refer to him as P, and in this Guide we call him the Priestly Writer.

2. The 'writer' of Gen. 2.4b—3.24, and other parts of Genesis. He probably did his work in the neighbourhood of Jerusalem. He uses the name *Yahweh* ('Jehovah') for God. For this reason some people refer to him as J. We call him the Older Writer, because he may have lived 950 or 900 years before Christ.

3. In Gen. 15, and also in other parts of Genesis yet another 'writer's' words were used. When he writes about God he uses the names *Elohim* and *El*. For this reason some people refer to him as E. We call him the Northern Writer because he probably did his work in the northern part of Palestine. He lived about 800 years before Christ.

We note certain things about these 'writers':

(a) The word 'writer' is put in inverted commas here because it does not refer to one single author. Most probably it was a group of people who did the work.

(b) We must not think that a group met together in order to write a story that had never been told. Their work was mainly to collect information and traditions which had been handed down by word of mouth for a long time. They probably also used some written documents.

(c) They did not only copy what others had said: they put their interpretation upon the stories which had been handed down.

40

Somebody collected together the writings of the Older Writer and the Northern Writer. Then, about 400 years before Christ, a group of editors made the work of all these 'writers' into the book which we call 'Genesis'. These editors, like the writers, interpreted what they had learnt, both from their own experience and the experience of their people, the Jews.

Genesis was not the only book to be 'edited' in this way. There is evidence to show that Exodus, Leviticus and Numbers were edited in the same way.

These, then, are suggestions about the way in which the Book of Genesis was written. They provide possible answers to certain questions, e.g. 'Why do we find one story in Genesis which seems to contradict another story in the same book?'

There are some readers who do not ask such questions, and it is not important for them to spend time considering the suggestions made in this Special Note. Moreover, these are only suggestions, and cannot be proved.

But those who do ask such questions should consider the suggestions very seriously indeed. They should accept them unless they have found another explanation which seems to be better.

Questions on Special Note B

1. Why do many people think that there was more than one 'writer' of the Book of Genesis?

2. What is the difference in meaning between the words 'writer' and 'editor' of Genesis as used in this Guide?

3. Complete each of the following sentences by choosing (i), (ii) or (iii):
(a) The earliest 'writer' of Genesis lived about
(i) 1,200 years   (ii) 900 years   (iii) 500 years before Christ.
(b) The 'editors' collected the work of the 'writers' about
(i) 400 years   (ii) 100 years   (iii) 50 years before Christ.

4. Give the names of two other books in the Old Testament which (in the opinion of many people) were edited in the same way as Genesis.

5. What would you reply to someone who said:
(a) 'I cannot trust the Bible any more because one chapter of Genesis contradicts another chapter'?
(b) 'I am totally confused by the suggestion that there were several writers of the Book of Genesis'?

4.1–15
Cain and Abel

OUTLINE

4.1–3: Cain is a farmer, Abel his brother is a shepherd who lives in the desert and goes from one place to another with his sheep. One day both make a sacrifice or offering to God, as a sign that they depend on Him for the success of their work. Cain offers something from the farm, and Abel offers pieces of meat from the first lambs to be born in that year. See Additional Note, Sacrifice, p. 160.

4.4–8: Abel's offering is acceptable to God, but Cain's is not. We do not know how they know that Cain's offering is not acceptable, but we know what happens afterwards. Cain is so jealous of Abel that he murders him.

4.9–15: After his terrible deed, Cain pretends to God that he does not know what has happened to Abel. God's reply is to say two things: (a) since Abel has no brother to act on his behalf, He will act for him; Cain is to be expelled from his work as a farmer and will, in future, wander about like a refugee (4.10–12); (b) but He will protect Cain and put a mark on him to show that he still belongs to Him (4.15).

INTERPRETATION

1. The chief reason why the editor has given us this story is that it illustrates what he has shown us in Gen. 1—3. This was: *Although human beings were made by God, they became separated from Him. They stand in need of rescue.* In Genesis we are shown three things:

(a) Human sinfulness: Cain, like Adam, is all humanity. His sins were jealousy and murder, the failure to be responsible for his brother (4.5–10): these are not sins of Cain alone, but of all of us. We may avoid murdering anyone, for fear of punishment, but we let resentment and anger grow within us (Matt. 5.21, 22).

(b) The result of sin. The result is painful: it is separation from God and from others (4.12–14). See Additional Note, Sin, p. 162. Cain became a 'wanderer'.

(c) God's mercy: Cain deserved to be killed, but God offered him forgiveness and promised to protect him (4.15).

In the days before this story was written down, there were probably other reasons why people liked to tell it to each other. It seemed:

(a) to explain why there is often enmity between settled tribes who farm the land and tribes who move with their herds from place to place;

(b) to tell them when people first offered sacrifices.

The writers of Gen. 4 have made this chapter look like a continuation of Gen. 3. But the chapter really refers to a much later time. The words 'whoever finds me' (4.14) show that by that time there were many other people living. This is also shown by the word 'city' in 4.17.

NOTES

4.1a. Now Adam knew Eve: In the Bible the verb to 'know' people is used in several ways. Sometimes it is used to mean to 'have information about' them or to recognize them, but often to 'be concerned about' or connected with them, to 'share life with' them. In this verse it means to have sexual intercourse with them. Thus people *know* other people with the whole of themselves, not only with their minds, eyes or ears.

If we have 'knowledge' of God, we not only think with our minds that He exists. We are also choosing to belong to Him, to be faithful and obedient to Him, to have a deep relationship with Him. See John 17.3.

4.1b. I have gotten a man with the help of the Lord: In Gen. 3 we read of the man and woman living as if they could be independent of God. But the words of this verse are a shout of joy from the mother that, *with God's help*, she has borne or 'created' a child. Whatever good thing we create, whether a baby or a book or a building, we do so in partnership with God the Creator. We are dependent on Him.

4.2. Abel was a keeper of sheep: We read here of work. Abel was a shepherd, Cain grew crops. As we saw earlier (p. 37), work is God's good gift. But it must be done within a harmonious community. Where there is disharmony (e.g. 4.5–7), work does not benefit the workers.

4.3, 4. Cain brought to the Lord an offering . . . and Abel brought of the firstlings of his flock: This is the first of many passages in the Book of Genesis where we read of people offering sacrifices to God. See Additional Note, Sacrifice, p. 160.

4.5. For Cain and his offering he had no regard: The writers do not explain why God did not accept Cain's sacrifice. Some people think that Cain was making his offering for one reason only, namely to increase his crop, and had no regard for God Himself.

4.6a. The Lord said: We have already seen that this story is important because of its teaching about human sinfulness and the mercy of God, rather than exact descriptions of what took place. Teaching of this kind does not change, and it is for this reason that people read the Bible today. See notes on 2.4b and 2.18. The teaching behind the words 'The Lord said' is that God in His mercy makes known His will to us in every generation. See Additional Note, Say, p. 162.

4.6b. Why are you angry? Cain is angry because God did not accept his sacrifice. But God does not just observe Cain's anger. He gets in touch with him and asks 'Why are you angry with Abel?' That is, 'It was not *his* fault that your sacrifice was not accepted. Consider what I am saying. If you do not, sin is ready to overwhelm you' (4.7). So God takes action to prevent Cain's crime. But Cain does not listen.

4.9. Am I my brother's keeper?: We saw in 1.26 and 2.15 that we must give account to God for the way in which we act towards God's created things and people. This is what Cain refused to do, even concerning his own brother. So many people today look at the very poor, those made homeless by war, or who suffer from incurable diseases, and say 'What have they got to do with me? They are not my concern. I do not belong to them.' See 1 Cor. 12.26.

The New Testament shows the full meaning of this 'giving account' to God: God holds us responsible in some way for all human beings because we belong to them, e.g.:

1. members of our own family (Eph. 6.4);
2. members of our own clan or caste or neighbourhood;
3. all fellow-Christians (1 Cor. 12.26); if there is suffering among Christians in Hong Kong, it concerns those Christians in Calcutta and Lagos and London who have heard about it;
4. those who are ill or without work. This is the meaning of the parable of the Good Samaritan, Luke 10.30–7.

4.11. You are cursed: That is, your action will bring suffering to you: God's world is a world in which evil actions have evil results. We cannot do evil which produces good results. The result of Cain's evil deed was that his land no longer produced crops and that he was without family or friends.

Those who edited this story were suffering oppression in exile in Babylon, and longed to be liberated. Some scholars think that they included this story to give a message to readers and others who were hoping for liberation. Their message was that oppressors (like Cain) will in the end be cast out. See Additional Note, Curse, p. 156.

4.15. The Lord put a mark on Cain: In spite of the sin of Cain, God promised to take care of him. We cannot escape from God, either from His judgement or from His love! The mark which He put on Cain was a sign of His promise and His care. It was not a mark to tell others that Cain was a murderer. (Perhaps the 'mark' which the writer had in mind was like the mark that some farmers put on cattle to show that they belong to them.) This is the wonderful thing that God does. He reaches out to rescue us even before we repent. Additional Note, Save, p. 161. A prison chaplain in London recently wrote this about two men who were in prison for serious crimes: 'Both men have really begun to understand that God has forgiven them and accepted them as belonging to Him. They are still surprised that this can be so.'

Questions on 4.1–15

Words:

1. The word 'know' in the Bible sometimes means (i) to have information about, and sometimes (ii) to be very closely connected with others, or care about them deeply. In the following passages which of those two meanings has the word 'know'? (a) Gen. 4.17 (b) Gen. 8.11 (c) 1 Kings 2.5 (d) Luke 16.15 (e) John 17.3 (f) 2 Tim. 1.12 (g) 1 John 4.7

Content:

2. What sort of work did Abel and Cain each do?

3. Why did they offer sacrifices?

4. (a) What does the 'mark' mean which God put on Cain?
(b) Why is it good news for us?

Bible:

5. Read the Additional Note on Sacrifice, p. 160. What reasons for sacrificing to God are referred to in each of the following? (a) Gen. 46.1 (b) Exod. 24.4–8 (c) Lev. 9.7 (d) 2 Chron. 29.31

6. What is the difference between Cain's words in 4.9 and the teaching of the following? (a) Gen. 1.26 (b) 1 Cor. 12.26

7. What teaching were the writers of (a) Heb. 11.4 and (b) 1 John 3.11, 12 giving concerning the story of Cain and Abel?

Application:

8. 'The result of sin is . . . separation from God and from others' (p. 42).
(a) What part of Gen. 4.1–15 shows that this is so?
(b) Give an example from daily life.

9. 'My brother's keeper' (4.9). Give examples of Christians who show that they are caring for people in need in another district or another country.

10. 'You are cursed' (4.11). See Additional Note, Curse, p. 156. What reply can you give to someone who says 'God cannot be loving if He curses'?

4.16–24
Cain and Civilization

OUTLINE

4.16, 17: Cain has now come to the end of his wanderings and has reached a country where there is a big population. He marries and then takes part in the building of a city.

4.17–22: The names of some members of Cain's family are given, and the occupations of three of them. These occupations are: looking after cattle, music, and metal work. Some of them have thus taken up new kinds of work.

4.23, 24: A song of Lamech, a descendant of Cain. Lamech boasts that if a neighbour hurts him, he will take revenge on him. His revenge will be far more severe than the revenge which God said would be taken on anyone who killed Cain.

INTERPRETATION

The editors of this passage did not intend it to be a continuation of 4.1–15; they are writing about a different time. Probably they were not the same as the editors of 4.1–15.

Again, this is not a passage simply about one man and his family, but about human beings. It is about people who are 'civilized'. Three signs of 'civilization' are given:

1. People are able to live at peace with others: e.g. in a city (4.17).
2. They are able to control their surroundings: e.g. by using iron (4.22).
3. They are finding new ways to enjoy life: e.g. by making music (4.21).

The writers seem to say two things about 'civilization':

(a) It can be good. They give us the names of Jabal, Jubal, and Tubal-cain because they regard them as people who have done great and good things. So in our own day Christians not only thank God for His gifts of rain and sun, but also for the gifts which come from Him through 'civilization': e.g. better health, improved food, better communications, i.e. more ways of meeting and understanding other people.

(b) Civilization also has dangers in it: it can bring evil. Cain's family was 'civilized' and 'progressive', but he was the murderer. And the member of his family who sang the terrible song of revenge (4.23, 24) was also 'civilized'.

In our own age, 'civilized' nations were mainly responsible for the two great world wars since 1914 and for the endless suffering which has resulted from those wars. And people from civilized nations are now spoiling huge territories of the earth and ruining their inhabitants in order to make profits for themselves.

Civilization' is thus neither good nor evil. What it does is to increase our powers. With these new powers we may do good or evil. If we are 'civilized', we are not 'better' people. We have more ways of being useful and generous, but we have also more opportunities for being greedy, dishonest and cruel.

NOTES

4.17. Cain knew his wife: See note on 4.1: 'Adam *knew* Eve'. The writers were here referring to a much later time, when there were enough people to fill 'a city'. This is the answer to those who say they cannot take the Bible seriously because there were no women for Cain to marry.

4.24. Lamech seventy-sevenfold: This verse shows what a great change Jesus achieved:

1. Here Lamech says, 'If anyone hurts me, there will be no limit to the hurt I will do him.' (Seventy-sevenfold means 'without limit'.)

2. Later the writer of Deuteronomy wrote, 'If anyone hurts one of your teeth, you can hurt one of his, but no more than one' (Deut. 19.21).

3. Jesus told Peter that if a brother hurt him, he should forgive him 'seventy times seven' (Matt. 18.21–2). So the thought expressed by Jesus is the *opposite* of the thought expressed by Lamech.

Questions on 4.16–24

Content:

1. 'The editors of this passage did not intend it to be a continuation of 4.1–15' (p. 46). What reason is there for thinking this?

2. Which verses refer to
   (a) people controlling their surroundings?
   (b) people living together in peace?

Bible:

3. What is the chief difference in thought between 4.16a and Ps. 139.8?

4. (a) In what way is the teaching of Jesus different from Lamech's words in 4.24?

(b) What enables Christians to do what Jesus says in Matt. 18.21, 22 (see Eph. 4.32).

Application:

5. Civilization 'can be good . . . it can bring evil' (p. 47). Give two examples each from your experience of
(a) good results of civilization
(b) evil results of civilization.

6. 'Cain knew his wife' (4.17). A famous writer mocked Christians and wrote, 'Your Bible is nonsense. Eve was the only woman in the world according to previous chapters.' What reply could you have given?

4.25—5.32
Seth and Salvation

OUTLINE

Here the editors of Genesis have put together two passages which give genealogies or lists of names of descendants of Adam.

4.25, 26: In these verses by the Older Writer we read that Adam had another son, Seth (in addition to Cain and Abel), and that Seth had a son, Enosh, which means 'will not live for ever'.

5.1–32: These verses are by the Priestly Writer; they too give the names of Seth and Enosh, and ten other names in addition.

INTERPRETATION

When we first look at this passage it seems to be nothing more than two lists of names. But it is much more than that. In it the editors show us that *God brings new hope to us at a time when we are corrupted by sin.* The birth of Seth is the sign of that hope.

1. In Gen. 4 we are reminded of human sin and suffering. Cain stands for sinners who oppress others. Abel stands for people who are oppressed by others. There seems to be hardly any hope that we can be saved from such sin and suffering.

2. At this point God brings Seth into the situation. Seth stands for all people who bring hope to others. We regard Seth as a sign of hope for these reasons:

(a) He was in the image of his father Adam, just as Adam was in the image of God (5.1, 3).

(b) He is 'appointed' or 'set apart' (the name Seth sounds very like the Hebrew word for 'appointed').

(c) He has a son, Enosh, who, it is said, was one of the first people to 'call upon God's name' in worship (see 4.26).

3. Seth is thus the first of that group of men and women who tried to remain faithful to God throughout the story of the Old Testament. In the list in this passage we find the names of the first ten of that group. If Christians want to discover the beginning of their Church, they can look back not only to the time when Jesus called His first disciples: they can look to this group of faithful people (Seth and his descendants) who are, so to speak, the ancestors of the Christian Church. St Paul supports this. In Gal. 3.7 he speaks of Abraham as the father of the 'people of faith', i.e. of the Church. We see in Gen. 10 and 11 that Abraham was a descendant of Noah, and in this passage Noah is a descendant of Seth.

4. The passage is therefore good news. From earliest times there has been a continuous line of men and women raised up by God to be faithful to Him. He saves and rescues, and He does this through people who are willing to be used in His service.

5. The passage is also a call to choice. The readers are asked to choose whom they will follow: those who, like Cain, rebel against God and become the destroyers, or those who, like Seth, obey God and are used by Him to build up what is destroyed, to save what is being lost.

A West African Christian interpreted the character of Seth in this way: 'We know that when we are among people who practise bribery we have to take a decision: e.g. in certain hospitals or among the thousands of young men looking for a job. We know that the custom of bribery destroys trust among people and destroys good work. We know also that we can help to build up our nation if we have the courage to refuse to take part in the custom.'

NOTES

5.24. Enoch walked with God; and he was not, for God took him: We cannot tell what the writers of these words thought. See also Heb. 11.5. But some Christians use the words to describe those whose prayer and trust bring them nearer to God, and who know that God will still keep hold of them after death.

5.27. The days of Methuselah were nine hundred and sixty-nine years: People often ask if the lists of names in Genesis are accurate. Was Methuselah really 969 years old when he died? Did the men really live whose names are given here?

If the interpretation given above is correct, then clearly the editors did not do their work in order to answer questions like these. They intended to give people a message which they needed much more than information about people's ages.

Therefore if we try to answer these questions we can only say that we do not know, and that it does not matter that we do not know. We can only note certain information on these subjects:

1. Our bodies are not capable of living to this great age today and there is no evidence to show that human beings' bodies in those days were very different from our own.

2. The lists in this passage are like a list which the Babylonians used. The Babylonian list is much older than the one in Gen. 4.25—5.32, but, although it is so old, it was not written down until after Genesis was edited. Perhaps both these lists had come from the same stories which had been handed down for very many years by word of mouth. But there is a great difference between the two lists:

(a) The list in 4.25—5.32 is used to bring us a message of good news; the Babylonian list is no more than a list;

(b) the age of each man in the Babylonian list is about 43,200 years!

3. The names seem to be signs or symbols rather than real names. Both 'Adam' and 'Enosh' (4.26 and 5.6–11) refer to all human beings.

4. In telling us about these people who lived to a very great age, the writers were telling us that God had greatly blessed them. Being very old was believed to be a sign of God's blessing.

Questions on 4.25—5.32

Content:

1. Read again 4.25—5.32. What do we learn about God from these verses?

2. Name one way in which the lists of names in 4.25—5.32 are different from the list which the Babylonians used.

Bible:

3. Read Gen. 5.1. In what other verse of Genesis have we read that God made man in His own image?

Application:

4. We have read in 4.25—5.32 about a situation where some people (like Cain) oppress others, some (like Abel) are oppressed, and some (like Seth) are raised up by God to bring hope into the world. Describe any situation like this in the world, either today *or* in the past. Explain:

(a) Who in that situation is the oppressor?
(b) Who is oppressed?
(c) Who is being used by God to bring hope?

5. What would you reply to someone who said that the Bible was worthless because it states that a man lived to be 969 years old?

6.1–4
The Forces of Evil

OUTLINE

We read in these verses that 'sons of God' came to earth and brought disorder and evil by having sexual intercourse with human women (6.2). The children who were born as a result were huge people, described as *Nephilim*, or 'giants', or 'mighty men' (6.4).

INTERPRETATION

1. The editors probably did not expect their readers to regard this story as something that really took place. In these verses they give no names of places or people. It is thus a different kind of story from the story of the Flood that follows it.

There are many stories in the world like this one, e.g. in Greek and Hindu folklore. Men began to tell such stories when they met very unusual people or things and they wanted to explain what had caused them. Probably, in this case, a tribe of unusually tall people lived in Palestine a long time before the Israelites went there, and other tribes said they must have been the children of gods or of some strange beings who were partly divine.

2. Why then did the editors of Genesis (writing a very long time afterwards) include the story here? The answer seems to be this. The story of the Flood in Gen. 6—9 shows that people were punished because of the evil in the world. These four verses are an introduction to this story. In them the writers say, in the form of a picture, '*Evil is greater and more serious than most people think*. It is a disease which spoils the whole created universe.'

3. We who read Genesis may have been puzzled at the extent of the evil in the world, and may have wondered why even the best actions can result in trouble as well as in good. Food and medicine were sent to a country whose people were starving; the result was only partly good,

for many more babies were born and the starvation increased. Scientists looked for new cures for a disease; but they produced not only a wonderful new cure but a new poison, a new way of killing an enemy. A good and brave man led his nation out of poverty into prosperity, but, although the people now live longer and have more to eat and to read, they also live more greedily and less happily.

We see that even the best forms of government and education and health services are not enough to save us from the power of such evil. Only God can save us from an evil as great as this.

4. When we read of 'half-gods' we are reading of a belief in the evil which is outside us humans. Jesus did not contradict this belief, but He taught that it is more important to deal with the evil that is in us. 'It is the things that come out of him that defile a man' (Mark 7.15, NEB). But the evil in us is so uncomfortable that we often try to escape from facing it by thinking of the evil outside us instead.

NOTE

6.2. The sons of God saw that the daughters of men were fair: Probably the story-tellers who spoke of these 'sons of God' thought of them as half-gods who brought evil into the world. They did not call them 'fallen angels', i.e. angels who disobeyed God and were punished by being sent to earth. In New Testament times some writers did believe in 'fallen angels'. See 2 Pet. 2.4, and Jude 6.

Some readers regard these 'sons of God' as setting an evil example to future generations of men, by treating women as nothing more than things which give sexual pleasure to men.

Questions on 6.1–4

Contents:
1. In what way is 6.1–4 an 'introduction' to the story of the Flood?

Bible:
2. What is the difference in meaning between 'sons of God' as used in 6.2 and the same phrase as used in Rom. 8.14?

Application:
3. (a) Tell any story you know from traditional folklore which describes 'gods' coming to mix with human beings.
   (b) Why do you think people continue to tell this story?
4. 'Even the best actions can result in trouble as well as in good'

(p. 52). Give an example from everyday life to show that this is true.

5. Read Mark 7.15.

(a) Give an example to illustrate the truth of this verse.

(b) Is it easier to think about the evil 'outside' you rather than the evil within you? If so, why?

6.5–10
An Introduction to the Story of the Flood

OUTLINE

This passage does not contain a story, but it prepares us for the story of the Flood. There are two parts:

6.5–7: God sees how wicked people have become. He sees that they do not deserve to exist any longer.

6.8–10: But God sees that there is one good person.

INTERPRETATION

1. *Human sinfulness*

We have already read of this in Gen. 3 and 4. We have to confess that Gen. 6.5 is true today; we are not what God made us to be. We are deeply self-centred beings. See Ps. 14.3.

2. *God's sorrow*

God is sad because of such wickedness (6.6). This is the meaning of 'He was sorry'. The word 'sorry' as used here does not mean that God was 'ashamed of having made a mistake'.

3. *God is creator and judge*

Because He is Creator He judges people who have misused His creation. (See note on 6.7a).

4. *God rescues a part*

But God is merciful, and He gives to a part of humanity another chance to live: notice the 'but' in 6.8. Noah and his family are a sign of the part which is rescued (their rescue will be described in the story of the Flood).

Through all the Bible we read of a small 'part' of God's people, which He rescues. In Isa. 10.20 they are called the 'remnant' or the few who were left over after judgement. In the Gospels we read of those who use the 'narrow doorway' (Luke 13.23, 24), i.e. the true followers of Christ. See Gen. 45.7 and Additional Note, Remnant, p. 160.

5. *Rescued for others*

God saves this 'part' in order that they may rescue others. This is not stated in these verses, but elsewhere in the Bible this truth is important. God chose Noah in order that, through him, human beings might in the future live as God means them to live. God accepted the obedience of Jesus, and, because of Jesus, we have been given an opportunity of following him. Jesus' obedience was 'for many' (Mark 10.45).

NOTES

6.6. The Lord was sorry: Were the writers wrong in using the words 'sorry, sad, grieved' to describe God's feelings? It is true that God's thoughts are not our thoughts (Isa. 55.8) and that it is a mistake to think of God as if He were a human being. But we do not read in the Bible that God is without feelings. Passages like Hos. 11.8: 'My compassion grows warm and tender', and Luke 15.7: 'Joy in heaven', are important.

6.7a. The Lord said, I will blot out man: This is the writer's interpretation of the Flood. He was thinking (1) that everything that happens is due to God's direct action, and (2) that all disasters are God's punishment for people's sins. But Jesus did not say this. Although He taught that God is a judge, He did not interpret disasters in that way. When a tower fell down and killed eighteen people, He said, 'This was not God's punishment for their sins.' Nevertheless 'you must repent of your sins' (Luke 13.1–5). See also John 9.1–3.

So we should not think of God as being 'hot-tempered' and in that spirit deciding to destroy sinners with a flood. God has created a world in which people, through their own sinfulness, pull down on themselves (and on other living creatures) a weight of destruction and suffering. For example, we can break God's laws and refuse to live at peace with others in our community. But if we do, we bring disorder and suffering on ourselves and on the community. See note on 19.25 and Additional Note, Judgement, p. 160.

6.7b. Man and beast: When we human beings forget God and go astray, e.g. when we are only interested in personal or family advancement, the rest of God's creation suffers. His whole creation belongs together.

6.8. Noah found favour: Like Adam and Eve and Cain, Noah represents ourselves. Stories about him are parables about God and

'God has created a world in which people, through their own sinfulness, pull down on themselves and others . . . destruction' (p. 54).

These people stand among the ruins of their homes, after race-riots.

human beings. He is everyone who follows God in so far as he understands God. See Rom. 2.14, 15. Noah was not an Israelite. Nor was he one of the patriarchs like Abraham.

Favour: When God 'shows favour' He is treating someone better than that person deserves. So in 6.8 the Older Writer tells us that God saved Noah, not because Noah had won his salvation, but because of God's favour or 'grace'.

The Priestly Writer was probably saying something different from this, for in 6.9 he writes that Noah was 'righteous', i.e. that he was saved because he was good.

These are two different interpretations and they stand for two different sorts of religion. The first is nearer to true Christian belief ('While we were yet sinners, Christ died for us', Rom. 5.8). The second is like the religion of those who try to earn God's love by doing good. Paul warns his readers against this religion in Eph. 2.8, 9: 'By grace you have been saved . . . and this is not your own doing, it is the gift of God.'

Questions on 6.5–10

Content:
1. For what purpose did God choose Noah?

Bible:
2. Each of the following pairs of verses contains an important truth. Say in each case what that truth is.
    (a) Gen. 6.5 and Gen. 4.8   (b) Gen. 6.6 and Hos. 11.8
    (c) Gen. 6.7 and Gen. 4.12   (d) Gen 6.8 and Isa. 10.20

Application:
3. Look at the picture and caption on p. 55.
    (a) Give another example from everyday life to show that 'God has made the whole world in such a way that people, through their sinfulness, pull down on themselves and others a weight of destruction' (p. 54).
    (b) What reply would you make to someone who said, 'God cannot love people if that statement is true'?

6.11—8.20
The Flood

OUTLINE

6.11–13: 'God said "I will destroy them."' ' The story begins with God's judgement of human beings, of which we have already been told in 6.5–7.

6.14—7.9: God tells Noah what he must do in order to be saved. He tells him how to make a kind of boat or 'ark'. The Hebrew word for 'ark' is the same as that used in Exodus 2 to describe the little boat of bulrushes by which the boy Moses was saved. It is different from the 'ark' or 'box' of the Covenant (Exod. 25.10–22). God tells Noah how to cover it, and which animals, birds and reptiles to take with him.

7.10–24: When the Flood begins, Noah and his family and the animals go into the ark and are safe because it floats on the water.

8.1–14: After a long time the Flood goes down, and they find that the ark has come to rest among the mountains of Ararat.

8.15–20: So Noah, his family, and the other creatures come safely out of the ark, and Noah sacrifices to God.

INTERPRETATION

1. We have already seen the interpretation of this passage in 6.5–7; but the editors probably wanted to show in particular the following two truths:

(a) *God is Judge:* The Flood came which caused so much destruction because of human wickedness. It was the result of God's judgement. See Additional Note, Judgement, pp. 156–7.

God did not only judge the people of long ago: we men and women of the twentieth century are as much under His judgement as the people about whom we read in Genesis. In Matt. 24.37–9 we are reminded of this. Sometimes we see clearly that disease or disaster has taken place as the result of human sin.

Many modern farmers in Europe have been feeding their cattle on a food mixture which contained the flesh of other animals, although grass and plants is the natural food for cattle. They have done this because it was cheaper. But as a result cattle died of 'Mad Cow Disease'.

But at the same time we must notice that there are diseases and disasters which are certainly *not* punishment. See note on 6.7a.

(b) *God is Saviour:* People were saved from the Flood because of

'Most of the story of the flood is about God saving' (p. 59).

These villagers are saving a little boy after winter storms in Italy.

God's mercy. This is the chief lesson of this passage. Most of the story of the Flood is about God saving Noah and those with him. Only a few verses tell of the destruction caused by the Flood. See Ezek. 33.10, 11 and Additional Note, Save, p. 161. A judge in Holland showed this sort of 'mercy'. He had to fine a poor unemployed man for stealing money. But he met him afterwards and put him in touch with someone who could give him work, so that he could pay the fine rather than go to prison.

2. The writers have handed down this story in order to proclaim *these* two great truths about God, not to tell us about floods long ago. To receive truths about God is the reason why we go to the Bible, just as we go to a bread shop to get bread, not to have a bicycle repaired. So if people ask 'Is this story true?' our answer is, Yes, we have found that its lessons are indeed true: God is indeed Judge and He is indeed merciful.

We sometimes forget this. Travellers have climbed mountains in the country which used to be called Ararat (today a part of Turkey) to see if they could find Noah's ark. They wanted to show that the story of the ark was true. They have not found the ark; but even if they had, the story would not be any *more* true for us than it is now. We would not trust the Bible any more than we do now. We would not know anything more about God and His will for us than we do now.

As far as we can tell, this is what happened: Many thousands of years ago (perhaps in about 4000 BC) a great flood, or several great floods, took place between the River Tigris and the River Euphrates, in the country now called Iraq. Stories about this flood were handed down by word of mouth for a very long time, and one such story was written down (by the Babylonians). Perhaps these stories became known to the Jews much later. Both the Older Writer and the Priestly writer of Genesis used a story of a great flood. Their stories of the Flood are like the Babylonian story in many ways. The editors of Genesis then used their stories to teach the great lessons about God, which they and their people knew to be true.

NOTES

6.13. I have determined to make an end of all flesh: 6.11–13 are a repetition of 6.5–8, and the reason is that the editor has combined two accounts. 6.5–8 come from the Older Writer, the rest of the chapter comes from the Priestly Writer. For the interpretation of this verse 13, see note on 6.7a: 'I will blot out man'.

6.14. Make yourself an ark: God did not rescue Noah and his family from the Flood by magically removing the water. We should not say that 'Noah was lucky to escape'. Noah lived through the Flood because he trusted God enough to do the work that was necessary before the flood came. God put it into his mind to make an ark and Noah set to work and made it. We remember Phil. 2.12, 13: 'Work out your own salvation . . . for God is at work in you.' God does not do for us what we can do for ourselves with the minds and skills He has given us.

Present-day Christians sometimes are disheartened by the amount of evil and suffering which is around them, personally and in their community. It feels like a flood. But, like Noah, they are not helpless. God can show them what action they can take, by working with other Christians and all people of good will, to resist evil and build up a just community. See 1 Kings 19.14–16.

6.17. I will bring a flood of waters: The writers of the Bible use the idea of 'water' or 'waters' in three special ways:

(a) as a sign of God bringing refreshment and new life (John 4.14);

(b) as a sign of God making clean and bringing forgiveness (1 Cor. 6.11);

(c) as a sign of something terrible from which it is God's will to rescue human beings; this is, of course, its meaning in this story (see also Matt. 8.24–7).

6.18. I will establish my covenant: A kind of covenant or agreement between God and man was mentioned in 4.15. Here (in 6.18) another agreement is mentioned, and this time the word 'covenant' is used. See Additional Note, Covenant, p. 155.

7.2a. Take with you seven pairs: Why do we read in 7.2 that 'seven pairs' of each creature were taken into the ark, but in 7.9 that only two pairs of each were taken? The reason is probably that 7.2 was in the Old Writer's story, and 7.9 was in the Priestly Writer's story. The editors have put both together in Gen. 7.

Another difference is that one writer says that the Flood remained for forty days (7.12), and the other says that it was there for 150 days (7.24). This shows that the editors were not aiming to give us accurate information on what took place. We should be very surprised if their stories were all the same.

7.2b. All clean animals: When God created animals He regarded them all as 'very good' (1.31). But the Jews called some of them 'clean' and others 'unclean', and did not eat those which they called 'unclean'. This custom was one of the chief signs that Jews were separate from non-Jews, or 'Gentiles'. The 'Gentiles' were regarded as 'unclean' because they ate 'unclean' animals.

Jesus reminded His followers of God's intention in the Creation: He would not call any animals unclean (Mark 7.14–19). So the first Christians were being faithful to Him when they refused to call any animals unclean and refused to regard Gentile Christians as being separate from Jewish Christians (Acts 10.9–16 and Gal. 3.28).

7.19. All the high mountains under the whole heaven were covered: Did the Flood really cover all the mountains of the world? Surely not. But we are not wise to spend time trying to find out the answer to this: e.g. by seeing if it would be possible for water as high as Mount Everest to exist all over the world at the same time. The editors were not aiming at giving us information of this kind. They were showing how very great was the Flood from which God rescued Noah.

8.1. God remembered Noah: This does not mean that God had forgotten or forsaken Noah until this time. Often, in the Bible, the words 'God remembered' mean 'God showed His mercy in a special way'. See Additional Note, Remember, p. 159.

Questions on 6.11—8.20

Words:

1. What is the difference between the 'ark' referred to in this story and the 'ark' referred to in Exod. 25.10–22?

Content:

2. What did God tell Noah to do, according to this story, in order to be saved?

3. Whom did Noah bring into the ark as well as himself?

4. (a) Why did Noah send a dove out of the ark?
   (b) What did Noah discover when the dove came back for the second time?

5. What is the modern name of the country in which the River Tigris and the River Euphrates meet?

6. What did Noah do as soon as he got out of the ark?

7. In 7.2 we read that seven pairs of each clean animal were going into the ark, but in 7.9 that only one pair went in.
   (a) Why do we find this contradiction?
   (b) Why did the editor include both verses?

8. 'Most of the story is about God saving Noah. Only a few verses tell of the destruction caused by the flood' (p. 59). Check the truth of this statement in the following way:
   (a) Make a list of those verses in which the writers refer to evil and its destruction, in the passage 6.11—8.20.
   (b) How many verses were there in that list?
   (c) How many verses are left?
   (d) Say in a sentence what these other verses are about.

Bible:

9. Say whether the writer, in each of the following verses, was using the idea of 'water' as a sign that God:

(i) brings new life, or

(ii) brings forgiveness, or

(iii) offers to save man from something terrible.

(a) Gen. 6.11—8.20   (b) Ps. 1.3   (c) Ps. 42.1

(d) Mark 1.8   (e) Luke 8.24   (f) Eph. 5.26

10. Read Matt. 24.37–9 and say what Jesus wanted to teach His hearers by the story of the Flood.

11. Read the Additional Note on Remember on p. 159. Then say whether the writer in each of the following verses is using the word 'remember' to mean:

(i) to hold in one's mind or to recall to one's mind, or

(ii) to show mercy in a special way.

(a) Gen. 8.1   (b) Gen. 42.9   (c) Exod. 2.24   (d) Matt. 16.9

(e) Luke 1.72   (f) Luke 23.42

Application:

12. If travellers found pieces of Noah's ark on a mountain in Turkey, would that make it easier to believe the Bible or to believe in God? Give a reason for your answer.

13. 'God does not do for us what we can do for ourselves with the minds and skills He has given us' (p. 60).

(a) In what way do we see the truth of this statement in the story of the Flood?

(b) Give an example from everyday life to illustrate it.

14. People have sometimes compared the Church to the ark.

(a) In what way is this comparison true and useful?

(b) In what way might it mislead us?

15. What is the difference between this story of a Flood and the many stories about floods in ancient times which we find in traditional folklore?

16. Many years ago a non-Christian wrote: 'The Bible shows that God cruelly destroyed most of the world with a flood. But Christians pretend that God is "loving" because a few people survived.' What reply would you make to that statement?

8.21—9.17
God's Covenant with Human Beings

OUTLINE

The writers here describe a meeting between God and Noah. It takes place after Noah has come out of the ark, and has offered a sacrifice to God. We consider the meeting in three parts:

8.21—9.1: God says, 'People are sinful, but I will make a "covenant" with them' (8.21b). 'I will not destroy them, but will protect them. I will bless them' (9.11). See Additional Note, Blessing, p. 154.

9.2–7: God shows Noah the laws by which people can live with other people and other living creatures. Keeping these 'laws' is the part which they take in the covenant.

9.8–17: The covenant is stated again. God says that the rainbow is a sign that He will keep His part of the covenant. It is His 'promise'.

INTERPRETATION

1. The great truth in this passage is that God is someone who comes to 'meet' men and women. He is someone with whom they can have 'conversation'. He is someone who has taken the first step in making an 'agreement' between themselves and Himself.

In using these words we do not mean that God is like a human being: we are using these words because we can find no better way to express our experience of Him. See Additional Note, Visit, p. 163.

2. God continually treats us *all* in this way. He was not making a covenant with one group of people only, or at one moment only. See 9.9: 'You and your descendants'.

3. This covenant with Noah refers to *natural* laws which we must keep. These laws are not the same as the laws of the various nations to which people belong today nor are they the same as the laws which God later revealed to His People, e.g. to Abraham and his descendants (Gen. 15 and 17). They are laws for people who have an elementary knowledge of good and evil (see Rom. 2.14). People keep these laws, not because they love their neighbours, but in order to avoid pain.

God provided these 'natural' laws so that human beings might be protected. We keep these laws when we avoid putting our hands into a fire. We must all live under these laws in order to survive, and so they are called 'natural' laws.

4. But *natural laws are not enough*, as we see in Gen. 12. God wanted His People to live as His sons and daughters who love Him. This is why He made *special* covenants with a special group of people,

63

'God is someone who comes to "meet" men and women. He is someone with whom they can have "conversation"' (p. 63). This student at the language laboratory at the Selly Oak Colleges, Birmingham, is learning with electronic equipment how to have conversation with someone who speaks a different language.

i.e. the Jews. In Gen. 12 and Exod. 19 we see the first two steps which God took. He took the most important step of all when He made the *new covenant* through Jesus (1 Cor. 11.25).

5. Christians live *under two covenants*. They are under God's 'natural laws', but they are also living under the 'new covenant' which He 'revealed' in Jesus Christ (Luke 22.20).

NOTES

8.21. The Lord smelled the pleasing odour: These words speak of God as if He were a man returning home and being happy to smell again the smell of his wife's cooking and the smoke of the fire. The same may be said of 9.16, which speaks of God as if He needed to look at the rainbow in order to remember His promise. Of course God does not need smoke to put Him into a generous mood, nor does He need to be reminded of anything He has done. God is *spirit* (John 4.24). But when we speak of God we have no words to use except the words that belong to our own world and our own human lives. What we must do is remember that they are symbols or picture-words, and see behind the words to the truth which is waiting for us.

Note: The editors have put together information from the Older Writer and the Priestly Writer, as he did in earlier chapters. This is the reason why 8.21 occurs again in 9.11.

9.2. The fear of you . . . shall be upon every beast: If we interpreted this wrongly, we might think that we were encouraged to be cruel to animals. But its real meaning is the same as the meaning of 'have dominion' (1.28b).

9.4. Its life, that is, its blood: See Additional Notes, Life (p. 157), Blood (p. 154). The Israelites thought of the blood of a living creature as a mark of its life. They also regarded sacrifice as offering 'life' to God. Therefore they must not drink the blood, but offer it to Him. Most Jews today will only eat meat from which the blood has been drained. Christians do not have to follow them, but we do believe all life, including our own life, belongs to God and is to be offered to Him.

9.6. Whoever sheds the blood of a man, by man shall his blood be shed: If someone kills someone else, that person has destroyed a creature made in God's image and has rebelled against God. So that person must be killed. If not, there is chaos in the community. That was a law at a time when there were no police and no law-courts. (But we cannot prove from this verse that 'capital punishment' is according to God's will today.)

Questions on 8.2—9.17

Words:

1. Which of these two words gives the better meaning of the word 'covenant'? (a) contract (b) expectation. Explain your choice.

Content:

2. What is the chief message of 8.21—9.17 which the writers wanted us to understand?

3. 'The Lord smelled the odour' (8.21).

(a) What other symbolic language do we see in this passage?

(b) Should we use such language when speaking of God? Give your reasons.

4. With whom did God make the covenant of which we read in 9.8–17?

5. What was the sign that a covenant had been made?

6. What did God promise after the covenant was made?

Bible:

7. What did the following people say about 'covenants'?

(a) Jeremiah in Jer. 31.31–4

(b) Jesus, according to Mark 14.24

(c) Paul in 1 Cor. 11.25

8. In 9.15 we read that God made a promise. After reading each of the following passages:

(i) say to whom God made the promise;

(ii) say what God promised to do;

(iii) give one way in which He kept His promise.

(a) 2 Sam. 7.8–16   (b) John 14.26.

9. 'God comes to meet men and women' (p. 63). From the following passages, say in what way God 'met' people: (a) Isa. 1.18–20   (b) Hos. 11.1–4   (c) John 1.14   (d) John 16.13

Application:

10. (a) In what way is baptism a 'covenant'?

(b) If it is a covenant, why are babies baptized in many churches?

11. 'Does God regard anyone as totally evil?' How does this passage help us to answer that question?

12. Give an example from daily life of two people making a covenant, and show how each can carry it out.

13. 'God provided these "natural laws" so that human beings might be protected' (p. 63). An example of a 'natural law', that we must not put our hands into a fire, is given in the notes above. Give two other examples.

14. 'We cannot prove from this verse (9.6) that "capital punishment" is according to God's will today.' What is your opinion?

9.18–29
The Weakness of Noah

OUTLINE

In these verses we read of what happened when the Flood was over.
9.18, 19: Noah settles on the land again with his three sons, Shem, Ham (who has a son, Canaan) and Japheth. According to 9.19 these three represent the different branches of the human race.
9.20–7: Noah is the first producer of wine, but he misuses it. On one occasion he gets drunk and lies naked in his tent. Ham discovers his sleeping father and behaves insultingly, and is severely rebuked by his brothers. When Noah wakes up, he curses the family of Ham ('Let Canaan be a slave to his brothers'), but blesses the others.
9.28, 29: Noah dies.

INTERPRETATION

1. Why did the editors of Genesis include this story?
It seems to contradict the description of Noah as a 'righteous man' (6.8). Three reasons have been suggested:
   (a) Perhaps they recorded it to show why the land of Ham's son, Canaan, lost its independence, and was occupied by the descendants of Shem (i.e. by the 'Semites', Arabs and Jews).
   (b) Perhaps the editors told it to explain how drunkenness began among the Canaanites. They wanted to warn their readers against the Canaanite religion, and so emphasized the parts of that religion which they regarded as wrong, e.g. men and women dancing and having sexual intercourse, believing that, through this, the gods or spirits would give them an increase of children and cattle. These customs influenced some of the Jews when they lived in the lands of the Canaanites.

(c) But probably the editors gave us this story in order to say this: 'We have shown you in Gen. 6—8 that Noah was a good man. Although he was described as "blameless" in 6.9, he was not perfect, for no one is perfect. But he listened to his conscience, and did his best. To some extent he knew the difference between right and wrong. He was a just man. He lived under the 'natural law' or 'covenant' which God made with all human beings (Gen. 8). But this 'natural' religion was not enough to save human beings from falling into a degraded way of living. We shall show you this same truth when we come to the story of the Tower of Babel. What people needed was that God should show them His will in a special way. And this is exactly what God did for Abraham and his descendants.'

2. *What has the story in 9.18–29 to say to the people of today?*

(a) God has given us, as he gave Noah, such good things as the instinct of sex, and the power to think and to imagine. To many of us he has given a fertile soil. Like Noah we have used these gifts to make good things for ourselves. Wine is one of these things, and so are many of the inventions of modern civilization. Like Noah (and like the family of Cain) we do not simply accept things as we find them. We work hard to improve the surroundings of our life, our food and drink, our health, our housing. We are 'progressive', and it is good to be progressive.

(b) But we, like Noah (and like Cain) continually misuse the good things God has given us and the good things we have made. For instance, people may get drunk because they are trying to forget a difficult problem. We do this because we have a weakness in us as well as strength. We forget that our own strength and goodness are not enough to help us to face trouble. There are many Christians who believe that the weakness of human beings is so great that no one should drink wine or any alcohol.

(c) We cannot be saved from disaster unless we accept the special message or 'revelation' which God has offered us. Relying on our own goodness is not enough. Living by the rule 'I will help you only if you help me' is not enough. Something more is needed.

(d) 'Something more' is just what God has provided. He began by giving His special revelation to Abraham: the whole of the rest of the Bible tells how He continued to give it. He gave it, for example, to the prophets, to those who wrote the Psalms, and above all, to His own and only Son Jesus Christ.

NOTE

9.25. Cursed be Canaan; a slave of slaves shall he be: Some of those who were engaged in the slave-trade used to point to these words and say, 'This shows that God intends the dark-skinned peoples of Africa to be slaves.' Some racists may still be saying this. Consider the following points:

1. Noah cursed Canaanites, not Africans. Canaanites, unlike most Africans, belonged to the race which we today call 'Semites'. See Additional Notes, Blessing (of God), p. 154; Curse (of God), p. 156.

2. The writers do not say that the curse was spoken by God, but by someone who had just woken up after being drunk.

3. Even if the writers had said that the words were spoken by God, that would not be enough to tell people how to behave towards others. We do not find out God's will by looking at just one verse from the Old Testament, but by a careful study of the whole Bible, especially of the words of Christ.

Questions on 9.18–29

Content:

1. Why did the editor include the story of Noah's drunkenness in the Book of Genesis?

2. Some people think that this story was handed down in order to explain why the land of Canaan was occupied by the Israelites. What part of the story leads them to think that?

3. Why did the Canaanites get drunk at certain times of the year as part of their worship?

4. 'This (natural) religion was not enough' (p. 68). Give two examples of God providing 'something more'.

Bible:

5. In what way was Noah like the family of Cain as described in 4.17–22?

6. In 9.18–29 we read of the weakness of a good man. What lesson do we learn from studying human weakness in each of the following passages?
   (a) 2 Sam. 11.1—12.13   (b) Mark 14.66–72

Application:

7. 'God has given us such good things as the instinct of sex. . . . Wine is one of these things. . . . But we continually misuse the good things.'
   (a) Do you agree or disagree with this statement? Give reasons for your answer.

(b) Give two other examples of 'good things' not yet mentioned and show in each case:

(i) a right use;

(ii) a wrong use.

8. 'People may get drunk because they are trying to forget a difficult problem' (p. 68). How can such people be helped?

9. If your father cursed you as Noah cursed Canaan, what would you feel? Explain your answer.

10.1–32
The World and its People

OUTLINE

In Genesis 10 the editors give us the information which had been handed down about the inhabitants of the world after the Flood. This information was as follows:

10.1: Noah had three sons, Shem, Ham and Japheth.

10.2–5: The family and descendants of Japheth lived in Asia Minor and other parts of Europe, e.g. in Javan (Greece), Tarshish (Spain), Kittim (Cyprus).

10.6–14: The family of Ham lived in Africa, e.g. in Egypt and Cush (this is probably Ethiopia).

10.15–20: The family of Ham's son, Canaan, grew in numbers and spread into other countries.

10.21–31: One place where the family of Shem lived was Elam (Iraq). We still use the word 'Shemite' or 'Semite' today to describe people who speak such languages as Arabic and Hebrew. Perhaps this information had been passed down from one generation to another because it gave an answer to the question, 'Why are races different from one another?' (The answer it gave was: 'Because they are all descended from different sons of Noah'.) But this is not the reason why the editors of Genesis have given it to us.

INTERPRETATION

Why did the editors of this chapter give us this list of races and nations?

1. To show that God's word 'to be fruitful and multiply' (1.28) had been fulfilled.

'Why are the races of humanity different from one another?' (p. 70). Whatever the reason, it is clear that peace can come only if one race respects the right of another race to be different.

Athletes from 35 countries took part in this Sports Festival in Japan. The fact that the competitors came from different countries made the events much more interesting and exciting for the spectators as well.

2. To prepare readers for the next part of Genesis (Gen. 12—50). In these later chapters (and in other books of the Old Testament) we see that God chose one people out of all the world in order that they should serve the others. See Isa. 42.6.

3. To show that God has a purpose for people of all races and nations and languages. In 10.1–32 there is no distinction between the 'good' people and the 'bad' people. There is no criticism of the Canaanites who are so often judged elsewhere, e.g. Ezra 9.1. The Israelites often forgot that God loved all nations and had a purpose for them. But there are passages in which we see God's love and purpose for all peoples very clearly, e.g. Isa. 42.5–9; Acts 17.26–28; Rev. 7.9–12.

NOTES

10.6. The sons of Ham: Cush, Egypt, Put, and Canaan: According to this verse the Canaanites were of the same race as the Hamites. But this is not so. As we have seen, the Canaanites belonged to the race which today we call Semites.

In the same way, we might think from 10.32 that all the nations of the world came either from Shem or Ham or Japheth: i.e. that all people are either 'Semites', 'Hamites', or 'Japhethites'. According to the place-names in 10.2–31, the writers regarded the 'world' as an area which stretched from Spain in the west to Iraq in the east, and from Greece in the north to Ethiopia in the south. But in fact there were other races living beyond that area: e.g. the races of India and China, of which the writers, it seems, did not know.

Questions on 10.1–32

Words:
1. (a) From what name does the word 'Semite' come?
   (b) What does it mean today?

Content:
2. 'Why did the editors give us this list?' (p. 70).
   (a) Which of the reasons given on pp. 70 and 71 do you think is the most important?
   (b) Give your reasons.

Bible:
3. 'There are passages in which we see God's love and purpose for all peoples very clearly' (p. 72). See Isa. 42.5–9, Acts 17.26–8,

Rev. 7.9–12, and from each passage choose one sentence which shows God's purpose for all nations most clearly.

Application:

4. 'All races and nations' (p. 72).

(a) Give examples of important differences between (i) two races; (ii) two nations or tribes who belong to the same race.

(b) Why did God make them different?

5. Why do people keep records of their ancestors?

11.1–9
The Tower of Babel

OUTLINE

11.1, 2: According to this story all peoples speak the same language, and they all settle in Shinar (Babylon).

11.3, 4: There they create a 'civilized' city in place of the old way of life, and build a tower that has 'its top in the heavens'.

11.5–9: But God sees that they have done this because of their desire to be independent of Him ('let us make a name for ourselves'), and because of their fear ('lest we be scattered'). He therefore puts a stop to their activity. At the end of the story there is confusion instead of order, and 'they left off building'.

INTERPRETATION

1. *The truth taught by this story*

(a) *Civilization:* We use this word to mean people living together (as in 11.2) and controlling their surroundings, making bricks instead of using stones (11.3).

There is no teaching in the Bible that 'old ways are better' or that cities and civilization and progress are wrong. But we do learn here that any civilized state or person will meet disaster unless they accept the authority of God. This is true of all states and people, whether they are called 'Christian' or 'secular'.

(b) *Independence:* But the desire to be independent of God is very strong. See 11.4, where we note that they wanted to make a 'name for themselves' i.e. a name that would be equal to the Name of God.

In Genesis we have already seen examples of people who tried to be equal with God or independent, e.g. 3.5. And today there is perhaps a greater temptation to live independently of Him than there has ever been. This may be because we have discovered how to control more and more of our surroundings through science. A schoolboy wrote, 'Each day we depend more on science and less on God: there will come a time when we shall have no need of God at all.'

(c) *God's Judgement*: If a people continue to be independent of God, disaster will follow. We can picture disaster as confusion and disorder (as in 11.7), or as the time when civilization comes to a stop (as in 11.8). If we refuse to follow the one God, then we lose the unity which God gives us, and disaster results. This is why disaster is called 'punishment by God' or the 'judgement of God'. See Additional Note, Judgement, pp. 156–7.

2. *Our own situation*

We must ask, 'Does this describe the way in which we live our lives in "civilized" countries? Does it describe the state to which we ourselves belong? Does it describe ourselves?' If we read the newspapers as well as 11.1–9, we may reply, 'Yes. We are like this, and disaster will come upon us.' And this may be so. The nations of the world may indeed destroy each other (e.g. by the use of nuclear weapons), so that life on the earth comes to an end.

But there is hope. The Bible does not end here. God has planned to rescue us out of disaster. In Gen. 12 we shall read of the step that God took in His work of rescuing by choosing Abraham. The rest of the Bible is the story of God continually calling to us, 'Why will you die? . . . Turn and live' (Ezek. 18.31, 32). The story of Pentecost (Acts 2.4–11) is a picture of the unity which God gives to those who are open to receive His Spirit. Someone has called Pentecost 'the story of Babel upside down'.

NOTES

11.1. The whole earth had one language: But in 10.5 we read that each nation had its own language. So there is a contradiction. What is the reason for it? It just means that 10.5 comes from the Priestly Writer and that 11.1 comes from the Older Writer. The editors use both stories. Since they did not aim to give us an accurate history, they are content to place these two different statements side by side.

11.2. Shinar: This is Babylon. Throughout the Bible writers use 'Babylon' as a sign or an example of a 'civilized' state in which citizens live without reverence for God, a state which rules cruelly over others by the power of its money or its weapons, a state which seems almighty but which meets disaster. (See Isa. 21.9; Rev. 14.8.)

11.4a. A tower with its top in the heavens, and let us make a name for ourselves: The people of Babylon used to build very tall towers called *ziggurats*, which looked somewhat like pyramids. Probably the tower referred to here was one of these *ziggurats*.

But 'its top in the heavens' refers to their depending on these high buildings rather than on God, as rich modern nations tend to do today. They wished to be 'on a level with God'. (See notes on 2.17 and 3.5.)
11.4b. Lest we be scattered: As we have seen, this independence resulted in disaster. But this verse 4b shows a second reason for disaster, namely the great fear that other nations will overcome them. Great civilized nations of today are spending millions of pounds on bombs and rockets because of their fear of each other, while the money spent on these weapons could provide houses and food for poor and hungry people.
11.5. The Lord came down: These words, like many sentences in 11.6–9, seem to speak of God as if He were a man, and as if He were living in the clouds. But we know that God is Spirit. The truth which lies behind these 'picture-words' or symbols ('came down') is that God is in our world and not distant from it.
11.6. Nothing that they propose to do will now be impossible for them: When we first read this verse we may think that God was afraid and envious when people became civilized. See note on 3.5. Perhaps some people who told this story to each other before it was written down did think this about God. But according to the rest of the Bible, God does not suffer from fear or envy, as we do. He wants us to grow more responsible and to develop the resources of the earth. But He hates to see us behaving as if we were God. This is because He loves us and knows that we need Him.

Questions on 11.1–9

Content:
1. For what two reasons did the people build their tower?
2. (a) What contradiction is there between 11.1 and 10.5?
   (b) Why does this contradiction exist?
3. What disaster resulted from the building of the tower?
Bible:
4. In what way is the story in Acts 2.4–11 'the story of Babel upside down' (p. 74)?
5. 'Tried to be equal with God' (p. 74).

(a) Make a list of phrases which have the same meaning from the notes on 2.17; 3.5; 11.4; and 11.6.

(b) Give an example of people doing this or trying to do this today.

Application:

6. If a world language took the place of separate languages, what would we (a) gain (b) lose?

7. 'There is perhaps a greater temptation to live independently of God' (p. 74).

(a) If this is true, what is the reason? If you think it is not true, give reasons.

(b) What can we do to resist that temptation?

8. 'The nations of the world may indeed destroy each other' (p. 74).

(a) How could this happen?

(b) What can we do to prevent it happening?

11.10–32
God's Choice of Abraham

OUTLINE

11.10–30: This is a list of Shem's descendants, repeating and continuing the list in 10.21–31. In these verses the editors extend the list until it reaches Abraham.

11.31, 32: Abraham's father, Terah, plans to take his family to Canaan. They leave their home at Ur, and settle for a time at Haran, where Terah dies.

INTEPRETATION

The writers have given us these lists in order to show that God was choosing one branch of the world's people, the Semites, to use them for His work. Now they give us the name of Abraham, as though they were saying, 'This is the man whom God has chosen out of all the Semites.'

NOTES

11.15. After the birth of Eber: Eber was the name of the tribe to which Abraham belonged, and from which the name Hebrews comes.

It was one of the many Semitic tribes who travelled about the deserts of the Near East for hundreds (and perhaps thousands) of years. Such tribes sometimes joined with other tribes and made a journey towards a country where there was more water. Perhaps this is how the 'Hebrews' reached the neighbourhood of Ur. We do not know where they came from.

According to Gen. 11, after living near Ur, the 'Hebrews', i.e. the Israelites, settled in Haran (550 miles away). The site of Ur is not far from the modern oil town of Basra in Iraq; the site of Haran is in the south of the country now called Turkey.

11.26. The father of Abram, Nahor, and Haran: Although the editors use the name Abram in parts of Genesis, the usual name in the rest of the Old Testament is Abraham. Haran was the name of both a place and a person.

Questions on 11.10–32

Content:

1. What is the value of reading the list of names in Gen. 11.10–30?

Bible:

2. In the following passages we read of people who, like Abraham, were 'chosen' by God. Say in each case
   (a) who they were
   (b) why they believed that they were chosen
   (c) what they were chosen to do.
      (i) 1 Sam. 10.20–24 (ii) Luke 1.26–38 (iii) John 15.15, 17

Application:

3. 'The man whom God has chosen' (see Interpretation).
   (a) Does God choose people in this way today? If you believe that He does, give an example.
   (b) How do such people know that God has chosen them?
   (c) How can they avoid feeling that they are 'superior' people?

Special Note C:
The Two Parts of Genesis

LOOKING BACK TO PART 1
(GENESIS 1—11)

THE GREAT TRUTHS

As we leave Part 1 of the Book of Genesis we bring with us certain clear lessons:

1. *All human beings are one*: The people about whom we have been reading were 'humanity' (God's 'Chosen People' were not mentioned until Gen. 11). Every truth in Genesis 1—11, e.g. that God creates and sustains us, is true about us, and about everybody. There is a real thing called 'humanity'. Such truths are far more important than the ideas which divide us. The first human beings are our ancestors and the ancestors of everyone.

In Gen. 11 we read of God choosing some people out of all others, but this was only in order that all people should be rescued.

2. *Everyone is in need*: We have seen that people failed to accept the authority of God, in spite of God's care and in spite of their own achievements. They failed in spite of their surroundings (of which Eden was a picture). They failed in spite of the civilization they made (of which the Tower of Babel was a picture). They failed in spite of God's punishment (of which the Flood was a picture).

This failure is human sinfulness, which we can compare to a disease. See especially notes on 2.17; 3.5; 11.4a; and 6.

3. *Everyone needs God*: The 'disease' was (and is) too severe for people to cure themselves. So God Himself took steps to rescue them from it. He began by choosing out certain people to do His work, of whom Abraham was one. So there is hope!

THE STORIES

All this has been shown to us by means of stories, i.e. in the only way in which such lessons could be taught. They are stories of things that really have happened, e.g. God has created people; people did sin; there was a flood; and there was a tower in Babylon. But the stories tell us very little indeed about *how* these things happened, for the editors were not writing a history textbook.

Also these stories tell us more about human beings in general than they tell us about individual people. We cannot say whether 'Noah' or 'Shem', for example, are the names of people who really lived. Perhaps each was an individual person, or perhaps each represented a whole

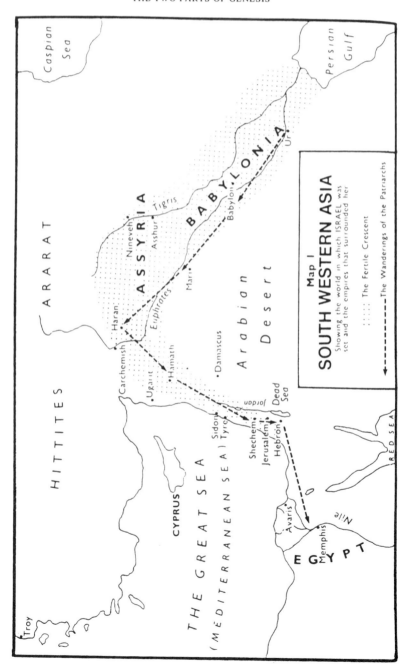

'There is a real thing called humanity' (p. 78).

What facts are true about all these different people, facts which are more important than the things which divide them?

race of people. It certainly was a custom to use the name of a single person when speaking of a whole nation or race or tribe.

LOOKING AHEAD TO PART 2
(GENESIS 12—50)

When we reach Gen. 12 we find that the stories are of a different kind. They tell us about people who, as far as we can tell, were individual persons, living at various times and in countries we can see on a map.

Abraham is the first of these people. The stories about him and about the other 'patriarchs' (Isaac, Jacob and Joseph) were probably handed down by men and women who were highly skilled in memorizing and telling old stories. Probably, at a later date, the priests preserved most of these stories and prevented changes being made. We can say, therefore, that these later chapters of Genesis tell us more about what actually took place than we can discover from Genesis 1—11.

This seems to be likely from the tools and other articles which archaeologists have dug up in the lands where the patriarchs lived. They were able to prove that such things had been used during the time of the patriarchs. Because of these discoveries they realized that people had in some ways been living as they are described in these chapters of Genesis. For example, at Nuzu in the north of Iraq, they found writings which describe the same customs of which we read in Genesis 12—50. See note on 16.3.

This is important, but we must not say that we know more than we really know. Even in the later chapters of Genesis no one can tell exactly what took place, for example, in Egypt when we read that Joseph saved the people from starvation. We do not know exactly what one person said to another, nor whether a name is the name of a person or of a tribe. We cannot know such things, because (a) the stories were probably not written down at all until about 800 years after the events took place; (b) the stories were not edited and included in the Bible until a long time after that.

However, we should not be troubled by the fact that we cannot tell exactly what happened. The editors' aim was to direct our attention on to something else: they saw that God Himself was active. And they wanted their readers also to see this. They wanted them to see that God Himself worked among His chosen people like Abraham, Isaac, Jacob and Joseph and their wives and families. God did His work through them in spite of their weakness and their mistakes. They were all parts of the long chain by which God was pulling humanity out of falsehood into truth.

Questions on Special Note C

Content:

1. What chief difference is there between Gen. 1—11 and Gen. 12—50?

2. Name *three* stories from Gen. 1—11, each of which illustrates *one* of the following:

(a) people failed to live as God intended in spite of His punishment;

(b) they failed in spite of the civilization they had made;

(c) they failed in spite of their good surroundings.

Application:

3. Look at the picture and caption on p. 80.

(a) What answer would you give to the question in the caption?

(b) Give two examples of things which harmfully divide people today.

(c) Give an example of something you can do now to show that there is such a thing as 'humanity' and that you believe in its oneness.

4. 'We do not know exactly what one person [referred to in Genesis] said to another' (p. 81).

(a) Do you agree? Give your reasons.

(b) Does it matter? Give your reasons.

(c) What would you reply to someone who said: 'We know what words were spoken by Abraham because God gave the writers of the Bible miraculous powers to write down His words long afterwards'?

THE BOOK OF GENESIS
PART 2

12.1–4a
God's Call to Abraham

OUTLINE

12.1–4a: Abraham was living in Haran when God told him to go to a new country. God promised to make him into a great nation, to bless him, and to use him to bring blessing to other people.

INTERPRETATION

In Gen. 10 and 11 the editors prepared us for stories about Abraham. Now, in Gen. 12—25 we read about him.

Understanding Abraham is important for the peace of the world. Christians, Jews and Muslims all regard him as their 'father'. See Isa. 51.2; John 8.56. Members of these religions are often bitterly divided, as are very many Jews and Arabs in Palestine today. But there can be hope for peace if we realize that we are all children of the same father.

Abraham was not an Israelite, although his descendants were called Israelites. He was a Semite who came from Mesopotamia (the land now called Iraq) and migrated to Canaan. He always regarded himself as a stranger and an immigrant in Canaan. (See note on 23.4.) There were weaknesses in his character (see 12.13) but there were great strengths:

1. He took action as the result of God's promises (12.4).
2. He was willing to be used by God to be of service to all nations (12.3).
3. He trusted and obeyed God, and bravely travelled to places far from his home (12.4a, 9).
4. He accepted God's covenant and lived by it (15.18).

NOTES

12.1. Go from your country: The journey was not Abraham's plan. God took the first step and started him on the journey. See 1 John 4.19: 'We love because He first loved us'. See also Rom. 4.17. So God began the long work of rescuing the human family from the results of its sin.

Abraham went because God had told him to go. But some things were probably happening at that time which also made him think that he should go. Perhaps he needed to find a country where there was more rain. We do not know. But even if we did know, for example, that he was looking for a land with more rainfall, that would not show that he was *not* called by God. Whenever we were trying to find out God's will, we have to consider many different circumstances.

12.2. I will make of you a great nation: This was God's promise, and surely astonishing to Abraham who had no children at that time. God was saying, 'Trust me and I will bless and protect you.' See Additional Notes, Blessing, and People, pp. 154 and 159.

But God's promise was that from Abraham a 'great nation' could be born. When God called people to do special work He intended them to work as members of a group. See 1 Cor. 12.27–9. A good Christian congregation is one where the ministry is usually shared, not left to one leader. See note on 2.18a. This 'great nation' was not the whole Jewish nation, but that part of the Jewish people who were faithful to God. This 'great nation' continued until the time of Jesus. Christians believe that when Jesus came, He came as a member of that same 'great nation' and that He developed it, so that those to whom He gave new life have become the Christian Church.

12.3. By you all the families of the earth shall bless themselves: (The exact translation of the Hebrew words is, 'Your Name shall be like a blessing on the lips of all people'.) God chose Abraham in order that He might, in the end and through people like Abraham, save the people of the world. So God was telling him to be of service to people outside his own family or clan. This has always been God's word to His people. But neither the Jewish people nor members of the Christian Church have always responded to this word of God. Too often they have worked only for the good of their own members. A great Christian once said, 'The Church exists chiefly for the benefit of those who are not its members.'

12.4a. So Abram went, as the Lord had told him: Here we see Abraham's obedience and trust in God. He went away from the encampment which was his home to a place of which he knew nothing. See Heb. 11.8. So also St Paul, having heard God's call, 'Go into the city' (Acts 9.6), obeyed God, although he did not know what would happen to him. See Acts 26.19.

Questions on 12.1–4a

Words:

1. Read the Additional Note on Blessing on p. 154.

(a) When did God give a blessing according to 9.1?

(b) When did God give a blessing according to 12.2?

(c) Who spoke a blessing on behalf of God according to 27.26–9?

(d) What does 'bless' mean in the Psalm: 'Bless the Lord, O my soul'?

Content:

2. How can understanding of Abraham bring peace to the world?

3. Why was Abraham surprised when God 'called' him?

4. What is the modern name for the country where Abraham lived?

Bible:

5. What truth about God can we learn from 12.2, Rom. 4.17 and 1 John 4.19?

6. What does 'faith' mean in Heb. 11.8?

7. 12.1–4a is about Abraham's 'call'. Read the following passages and say in each case (a) whom did God call? (b) what did God call them to do? (c) what was their response?

Exod. 3.6–11; Mark 2.13; 14 Acts 9.3–8

Application:

8. 'The Church exists chiefly for the benefit of those who are not its members' (p. 84). To what extent is this true?

9. 'Ministry is shared' (p. 84).

(a) Is it being shared in congregations which you know?

(b) Should it be shared?

(c) How far is 1 Cor. 12.27–9 a useful guide?

10. A reader of the note on 12.1 said, 'Either Abraham went away because there was a shortage of water *or* because he had a call from God. I can't believe both of those.' What is your opinion?

12.4b—14.24
The Promised Land

OUTLINE

This long passage contains several different stories. The editors have grouped them together here because all of them are about the Land of Canaan which God promised to Abraham and his descendants.

12.4b–9: The promise: Abraham leaves Haran and travels south until he reaches the hilly district of Shechem, now called Nablus. Here he worships God at the 'Teachers Tree', a sacred tree where the Canaanites probably obtained advice from a 'medium' about the future. Here he receives a promise from God: God will lead him and his descendants, so that they will have this land as their own. So Abraham builds an altar to show that this God is his God, and later he does the same near Bethel.

12.10–20: The journey into Egypt: in a time of famine Abraham goes to Egypt. He is afraid that the Egyptians will kill him in order to take his wife, so he pretends that she is his sister. As a result, Sarah is taken for a time into the king's (Pharaoh's) harem, and Abraham is not killed. Later they return to Canaan. Compare 26.7–11.

Gen. 13: Lot and Abraham: Abraham and his son-in-law, Lot, have so many cattle when they are living near Bethel that the land cannot support them all. Abraham, as the senior, suggests that each should live in a different part of the country, and invites Lot to choose a district. Lot chooses the valley, so Abraham has the high ground. From the hills Abraham can see much of the land of Canaan, and God tells him a second time that it will be for him and his descendants.

14.1–12: 'Kings' or tribal chiefs go to war.

14.13–16 and 21–4: Abraham rescues Lot from the king who had captured him.

14.17–20: Abraham meets Melchizedek, the priest and king of Jerusalem.

INTERPRETATION

The special truth about God which we can see behind these stories is that He makes promises and keeps them. We read of one promise in 12.7, and of others in 13.15; 15.7; 15.18; 17.8 etc. When He promised to give the 'land of Canaan' (12.5–7) to Abraham and his descendants, He was promising them two things:

(a) Surroundings which would be helpful to Abraham. See note on 12.7a below.

(b) His continual care. When Abraham went to Egypt to find food he was in danger from the Egyptians. But God had promised to look after him, and he came safely out of Egypt.

There are small groups of Christians all over the world who go on meeting together although they are a minority in their district, because they believe that they belong to God and that He will keep His promises and look after them, e.g. one little meeting of Christians in Northern Nigeria, who live in an area where everyone else is a Muslim.

NOTES

12.6. At that time the Canaanites were in the land: These words were written *after* the Canaanites had ceased to control the land and the Israelites had come in. This passage therefore could not have been written by Moses, for he died before the Israelites were in control of the land. (This does not surprise us: we do not read in the Book of Genesis itself that Moses wrote it. But when the Old Testament was translated into Greek, someone wrote the words 'The First Book of Moses' at the beginning of Genesis.)

12.7a. To your descendants I will give this land: (This 'land' was Canaan. See 12.5.) The Jews who collected together these stories and interpreted them out of their experience were exiles in Babylon (587–539 BC). In Babylon they had no land of their own, and they repeatedly drew attention to God's promise to give land to Abraham's descendants. See Gen. 13.15; 15.7, and very many other verses.

Today many people ask questions. For example: Who are Abraham's descendants? What is that land? Very different answers are given by different groups of people:

(a) Most religious Jews (and those Christians who follow them) say that modern Jews are those descendants, and that 'land' means territory in South West Asia. They add that the establishment of the State of Israel in 1948 was the fulfilment of God's promise to Abraham.

(b) Arabs point out that they too are descendants of Abraham. See interpretation on p. 83.

(c) Many Christians follow Paul's words in Rom. 9.6 and Gal. 3.7–9 and 29. Paul showed there that Abraham's descendants are not only Jews, but all those who have faith similar to Abraham's. Christians come to faith when they receive Jesus Christ. Thus 'land' does not now mean 'territory', but whatever the faithful need in order to keep faithful to God. The interpretation of the word 'land' is different because of Jesus Christ.

12.7b. He built there an altar: This altar was at Shechem; Abraham built another near Bethel (12.8) and another at Hebron (13.18). Probably he did not construct new altars, but used places where Canaanites had worshipped other gods and spirits.

When the Israelites used such altars, they sometimes worshipped the god or gods worshipped by pagans at that place (see 14.20), sometimes they worshipped their own Lord. Many centuries later the altars were used by those who knew that there is only one God.

Something like this has often occurred since that time also. Christians in their worship have used buildings or customs or language which had previously been used by pagans. We keep Christmas on 25 December, a day which pagans had previously kept as the feast of the planet Saturn. In many languages Christians use the same word for God ('Allah') which their Muslim neighbours use, but they put new meaning into the word.

12.13. Say you are my sister: The teaching in 12.10–19 is that God was taking care of Abraham in Egypt. Many readers of this verse condemn Abraham for telling a lie. Others think that we should not condemn him, since he was afraid they would kill him. But one student said, 'If Abraham told a lie, why should not I?' Whatever is our response to this verse, we need to remember that Abraham had not received the teaching of Jesus.

13.4. Abram called on the name of the Lord: That is, Abraham worshipped God. The 'Name' of God means His character. See Additional Note, Name, p. 158.

13.11. Lot chose for himself all the Jordan valley: Lot chose the fertile land which seemed at first sight to be the rich land, but in the end he found that it was dangerous (see 19.1–11). He made a mistake. But he could not know what would happen to this land, and he did not know that the people of Sodom were evil. But in the Bible Lot's action is used as a sign: it is used to show that someone without faith considers what is good at the present moment and does not consider what will be best in the end. We think of Jesus' parable of the Rich Fool (Luke 12.15–21).

14.18. And Melchizedek king of Salem brought out bread and wine; he was priest of God Most High:

Salem: This is the place of which Melchizedek was 'king' and priest. It was afterwards named Jerusalem. Here David built his city and Solomon built the Temple. Here Jesus died and was raised to life. Today it is a modern city. But usually the writers of the Bible use the word 'Jerusalem' as more than the name of a place; they use it as a sign, a sign that God is present with His people.

Melchizedek: We learn from Psalm 110 that the Messiah, or God's Anointed One, will not only rule as king, but that he will also be a priest, like Melchizedek (13.4).

The writer of the letter to Hebrews also mentions Melchizedek. He says in Hebrews 5—7 that Christ is a priest as well as being king. But, he says, Christ is not a priest like the Jewish 'priests of Levi' who were given authority in the time of Moses. Such priests were only human beings; their work will not continue for ever; their sacrifices in the Temple did not in fact lead to the forgiveness of our sins. Christ, on the other hand, was more than an ordinary priest; He was a priest for ever; He was a priest through whose loving sacrifice of His life sins really are forgiven. Then the writer of Hebrews says, 'Christ is like Melchizedek who was a king and priest, but not a priest like the priests of Levi.' See Heb. 7.11, 26. What do we say to this?

(a) We do believe that our sins can be truly forgiven through Christ. But our reason for believing is not that the writer of the letter to Hebrews says that He is like Melchizedek.

(b) Nevertheless, this teaching in Hebrews 5—7 is important. In many branches of Christ's Church there are people who are called 'priests' because they speak to God for us and speak to us for God. They do not continue the work of the 'priests of Levi', for they are people through whom the benefits of Christ's sacrifice can come to us. But Christ's sacrifice was not a sacrifice like the sacrifices offered by the priests of Levi: it was of a different sort.

Questions on 12.4b—14.24

Words:

1. Read the Additional Note on Name, p. 158. Then read Gen. 2.20, Psalm 96.2 and John 1.42, and say which one of those verses best illustrates each of the following statements:
   (a) Giving a name is having power over the other.
   (b) Giving a new name is giving increased responsibility.
   (c) Speaking of God's Name is speaking of His character.

Content:

2. Why did Abraham (a) go to Egypt (b) pretend that his wife was his sister? (c) suggest to Lot that they should live in different territories?

3. What double promise did God make to Abraham?

4. When did people first call Genesis 'The Book of Moses'?

Bible:

5. Which of God's promises is contained in all of the following verses: Gen. 12.7; 13.15; 15.7; 15.18; 17.8?

6. Read Gen. 14.18, and Heb. 5.5, 6; 5.10; 6.20; 7.1–3. Why did the author of the letter to the Hebrews compare Jesus to Melchizedek and *not* to the priests of Levi?

Application:

7. Different interpretations of 12.7a are given on p. 87. With which one of them do you agree? Give your reasons.

8. In many parts of the Church, ordained ministers are called 'priests' (as in 14.18) and the table used at Holy Communion is called an 'altar' (see 12.7).

(a) Why do those churches use those words?

(b) What does your local congregation teach about this?

(c) Give your own opinion on the use of those two words in Christian churches.

9. We read on p. 88 that people who believed in one God used altars which had previously been used by worshippers of other gods.

(a) What words, buildings or customs which have once been used by non-Christians in your country do Christians use today (if any)?

(b) When, if ever, is it right to do this?

15, 16, 17
God's Covenant with Abraham

OUTLINE

15.1–6: God promises Abraham that he will have a son of his own and many descendants. Abraham believes that it will be so.

15.7–21: God makes a covenant with Abraham by means of a sacrifice. In the covenant God promises again to give the land of Canaan to Abraham's descendants.

Gen. 16: Sarah, who has not had a child, offers her slave-girl Hagar to Abraham so that in this way he may have a son. But when Hagar is about to have a child, there is quarrelling between Sarah and Abraham and between Sarah and Hagar. Hagar runs away, but is told by God to return. She comes back and her son Ishmael is born.

17.1–14 and 23–27: This is a second account of the covenant. In this account God gives Abraham his new name, and the sign of covenant is circumcision.

"The Covenant is like an agreement" (p. 93).

When a customer bargains with a trader, as this woman is doing with a shoemaker in the Caribbean, they are making a kind of covenant. In what ways is this kind of covenant *unlike* the Covenant which God made with Abraham?

17.15–22: Again, God promises that Abraham shall have a son by Sarah, but Abraham does not believe Him.

INTERPRETATION

In these chapters the chief subject is the special covenant which God makes with Abraham. See note on 15.18. Then the editors have given us two different stories about this covenant. In Gen. 15 the Older Writer tells us that sacrifice was part of the covenant. See note on 15.9. But in Gen. 17 the Priestly Writer says that circumcision accompanied the covenant. See note on 17.11.

This covenant took place about 1,700 years before Christ and by it Abraham knew that he was joined in spirit with God. But the passage has been handed down to us because it also shows that all God's servants can be joined in spirit with God. When Christians use the well-known Methodist prayer, 'Lord, You are mine and I am yours. So be it', they are taking part in a covenant with God. See Rom. 4.23.

NOTES

15.6. He believed the Lord; and he reckoned it to him as righteousness: St Paul in Rom. 4.9, 22–5 has interpreted this for us. Abraham was 'righteous' in only one way, namely in his 'believing', his trust, his dependence on God's mercy. He says (Rom. 4.23, 24) that this is the only reason that God accepts us. We cannot earn His approval. We depend on His grace, which we have not deserved. See also Gal. 3.6–7.

In other ways Abraham was not a very 'righteous' person. Even if we do not think that his lie to the king was sinful (12.13), he was content to send his own wife to be one of the king's wives (12.14) in order to save his own life. According to 16.2 he listened to his wife rather than to God, and took her slave-girl as a second wife for himself (16.3). He laughed when God promised him a son by Sarah (17.7). We can follow him in his 'belief', his dependence on God's mercy, but should *not* do so in many of the things which he did.

15.9. Bring me a heifer: Here, as in 15.10 and 17 we read of the custom by which two people made a covenant by means of a sacrifice. They did this because in the eyes of the Israelites the blood contained the life of a living creature. Then those who were making the agreement stepped in between the pieces of the animals whose blood had flowed out. They believed that in this way they would be connected with each other because each of them was now connected with the blood and the life of the animals. In this story only God stepped between the pieces, and the sign of God was a smoking clay fire-pot and a flaming torch.

This story is not easy to understand, but it prepares us for the passage in Exodus 24.3–8 where another Covenant between God and His Chosen People is made by means of a sacrifice. Jesus probably had this chapter of Exodus in mind when He said, 'This is my blood of the new covenant which is poured out for many' (Matt. 26.28). See Additional Note, Sacrifice, p. 160.

15.18. The Lord made a covenant with Abram: We saw in Gen. 9.8–17 that God made a covenant with all the peoples of the world when He made it with Noah. Here in Gen. 15 and 17 the covenant is with Abraham and his descendants. For this word 'descendants' see note on 12.7a.

This covenant was a sign that God had a relationship with Abraham which He did not have with other people. The headmaster of a boys' school had one of his own sons at his school. He did not show him any favouritism, and sometimes seemed to treat him more severely than he treated the others. But the relationship with his son was different. This may be what Christians mean when they say that God has a covenant with them.

Thus the covenant is like an agreement or relationship between two people; but the two people in this covenant are not equals. God offers to make this covenant out of His great mercy: Abraham's part is to accept it and obey.

In all covenants each person must take some part. From this passage we learn that Abraham's part was to trust God. (We are not told that he made any promise to God, although God made a promise to him.) See Additional Note, Covenant, p. 155.

16.3. Sarai, Abram's wife, took Hagar . . . and gave her to Abram her husband as a wife: The editors of Genesis have told us about Abraham taking a 'second wife' to help us to understand the meaning of 'faith'. God promised to give Abraham a son by Sarai (15.4) and Abraham showed faith in Him. But later his faith and his wife's faith failed (16.3) and they decided to get a son by another way. By their action they were saying, 'God is not giving us a son, so let us get one without His help.' (But unhappiness resulted. See 16.4–6.) At that time there was a custom for a childless wife to provide her husband with a slave-wife. Writings have been dug up in Iraq which belong to the time of Abraham, which describe this custom. See also 25.1.

But Christians are not free to follow Abraham's example. They have traditionally based their teaching on verses like Eph. 5.33 and Matt. 19.5, and have seen marriage as the union of one husband to one wife.

17.11. You shall be circumcised . . . a sign of the covenant: The earlier account of the making of the covenant came from the Older

Writer. According to him Abraham's part was simply to have 'faith'. But the account in Gen. 17 comes from the Priestly Writer and he seems to teach that faith is not enough, and that people are joined to God in a covenant by keeping the ritual of circumcision. We see here the way in which the Jewish religion, under the influence of the priests, could easily become a religion of earning God's approval by performing ritual. See Additional Note, Circumcision, p. 155.

Questions on Gen. 15, 16, 17

Words:

1. 'This is my covenant . . . between me and you' (Gen. 17.10). Which three words of the following could be used in place of the word 'covenant' in that sentence without changing the meaning?
agreement bond commandment contract exhortation pact

Content:

2. According to Gen. 15, 16, 17, God made a covenant with Abraham by means of two different signs. What were they?

3. What is the chief difference between the covenant between God and Noah and the covenant between God and Abraham?

Bible

4. Read Gen. 15.6. What teaching did Paul give us when he interpreted that verse in Rom. 4.3, 9, 22, 23?

5. Read the Additional Note on Circumcision, p. 155. What single lesson do we learn from Jer. 4.4 and Rom. 2.29?

Application:

6. Abraham had two wives.

(a) Why do most churches forbid polygamy?

(b) How would you reply to someone who said that since Abraham had two wives, there is no law against it?

(c) If a polygamist becomes a member of a church, how should the church treat his wives?

7. 'The Lord said' (15.13). 'The angel said' (16.7).

(a) What is the meaning of the word 'said' in those sentences?

(b) How does God 'say' things to us today? Give an example if possible.

8. Circumcision was one way in which the Israelites made themselves 'distinctive' from others. What are the advantages and disadvantages of Christians behaving in 'distinctive' ways?

18 and 19
The Promise of a Son

OUTLINE

Although some of the stories we read here are about the evil of Sodom, the writers chiefly draw our attention to God's promise to give Abraham a son.

18.1–15: The Promise: God and two of His angels come to Abraham and Sarah. God says again that they will have a son. But Sarah cannot believe it.

18.16—19.38: The evils of Sodom: God tells Abraham that Sodom will be destroyed because its people are so wicked. Abraham begs God to save it if He can find ten good people there (18.16–33).

Abraham's nephew, Lot, lives in Sodom and is told by God what will happen. Even while God is with him, the people of Sodom show how wicked they are. Lot and some of his family escape death, but his wife does not (19.1–26).

Then the towns are destroyed (19.24–8). Lot's two daughters marry their father, believing that unless they do so there will be no more People of God to inhabit the world (19.29–38).

INTERPRETATION

1. At first there seems to be nothing more here than a collection of stories about the wickedness of men and women: Sarah laughs at God (18.12); she lies and says she did not laugh (18.15); Lot offers his daughters to the wicked men of Sodom (19.8); his daughters make him drunk and then have sexual intercourse with him (19.32). Some readers who open the Bible at this passage may decide that the Bible cannot help them to live a Christian life.

2. But there is a different way of reading it. The message behind the stories is the message of the whole Bible, namely that people have failed so badly in the way in which they live, that God Himself must rescue them. He will do this by means of a Chosen People. Thus:

The message of 18.1–15 is: 'Sarah will have a son, and God still promises to raise up a Chosen People, beginning with the birth of this son.'

In 18.16—19.38, we are reminded why God had promised this. It was because people were living, and still live, so evilly. (Sodom is an example of the evil.) This is why God had to begin the work of rescuing us. (But sin was followed by disaster, and only a few people were saved.)

95

NOTES

18.1. The Lord appeared to him: The writers of this story wanted their readers to learn this lesson: 'God is not apart from us men and women: He makes His will known to us.' (People did not fully understand this great truth until Jesus came and showed what God is.)

But the story itself is difficult to understand. It seems to say that God came in the form of a man (18.1); that two angels who also looked like men came with Him (18.2); and that they all ate (18.8). This is symbolic or picture language of the sort we found in 3.8. See Additional Note, Angel, p. 153.

18.14. Is anything too hard for the Lord? If a woman as old as Sarah can have a child then nothing can be too hard! All through the Bible God seems to do His work at times when people do not expect it: Sarah had expected the child when she was young. And God does His work in ways which seem impossible to human beings, e.g. He chooses the little family of Abraham instead of the great nation of Babylon. This is what Mary sang in her Magnificat (Luke 1.51–3).

18.23. Wilt thou indeed destroy the righteous with the wicked? This is part of the prayer which Abraham offered for the people of Sodom. At first it looks as if Abraham is being more merciful than God, but this is not so. God agrees that Sodom will not be destroyed if He can find even ten good people in it. We have seen before that God works in this way: in the story of the Flood the human race was given a new beginning because there was one good person, Noah. So, in the time of Jesus Christ, there was only One perfectly good Person: but for His sake we are all given a chance to be rescued.

We also notice that Abraham was praying for people who were not Israelites, that he prayed with humility (18.27), and as persistently as the friend in Jesus' parable (Luke 11.5–13).

18.30. Let not the Lord be angry: See Additional Note, Anger (of God), p. 153.

19.25. He overthrew those cities: Sodom was destroyed by an earthquake or by the eruption of a volcano, though we do not know when this destruction took place.

A question which readers may ask about the destruction of Sodom and Gomorrah is one which we have already asked about the Flood: 'Was it caused by God in order to punish the wicked?' We may also ask this question concerning other stories in Gen. 18—21, e.g. God's angels striking the men of Sodom with blindness (19.11); God destroying all the people of Sodom (19.24, 25); God agreeing that Hagar and Ishmael shall be driven into the desert (21.12). See note on 6.7a. There are two answers to this question.

(a) One answer is: the editors of Genesis thought that, in some cases at least, God actually caused the disaster because of people's wickedness. That was their interpretation. Isa. 13.19 and Amos 4.11 also suggested this answer.

(b) A different answer is: according to Luke 13.1–5 and John 9.1–3 Jesus taught that God does not rule His world in this way.

Many natural disasters occur, especially earthquakes, which are not caused by the sin of men. God does punish us for sin. Innocent people do suffer along with guilty people just because human beings belong to each other. But God judges and punishes by creating and allowing a world in which people prepare disaster for themselves. See the Note on 6.7a. According to Luke 19.42 Jesus said, 'Would that . . . you knew the things that make for peace', i.e. 'Do you not see that the way you are living cannot bring peace? It must lead to disaster.'

Jesus used this story of the destruction of Sodom as a picture of the judgement of God, but He was speaking of the *Last* Judgement. He did not use it as a picture to describe what God does during our lives.

19.26. Lot's wife . . . became a pillar of salt: As Christians we should not say that God (who is love) caused the death of Lot's wife simply because she turned round. (Jesus used this event to show that people must be ready for His Coming. See Luke 17.32.)

Questions on Gen. 18 and 19

Words:

1. Read Additional Note on Anger, p. 153, and the following passages, saying in each case
  (a) who made God 'angry';
  (b) why God was 'angry';
  (c) what resulted (or was expected to result) from His 'anger'.
Gen. 18.30   Matt. 3.7–10

Content:

2. What promise did God give to Abraham and Sarah?

Bible:

3. In what way is the message of Gen. 18.14 like the message of Luke 1.51–3?

4. Abraham prayed for people in Sodom (18.23). In the following passages we read of people praying. Say in each case whether it was a prayer of thanksgiving, or confession, or asking for themselves, or intercession: (a) 18.23–32 (b) 20.4, 5. Say also whether it was the sort of prayer which a committed Christian would make.

Application:

5. (a) Why did the editor of Genesis give us so many stories of people wickedness?

(b) Why do editors of newspapers give us so many stories of people's wickedness?

(c) Are you able to read stories of wickedness in the newspapers with the same faith and understanding with which you read such stories in Genesis? Give reasons for your answer.

6. In 18.1–8 and 19.1–3 we read of Abraham and Lot offering hospitality to visitors.

(a) Compare the way in which they offered hospitality with the way in which you offer it today.

(b) Is giving hospitality a Christian duty, or nothing more than an old custom? (See Heb. 13.2.)

20 and 21
The Birth of the Son

OUTLINE

Gen. 20: God protects Abraham: Abraham goes to the south of Canaan. He is afraid that the king may kill him in order to take his wife, so he says that Sarah is his sister. The king takes Sarah into his household, but God tells him to let her return to Abraham.

Gen. 21: The Birth: Now at last a son, Isaac, is born to Abraham and Sarah (21.1–7).

But as Isaac grows up Sarah says that Ishmael and his mother Hagar must go away. God agrees that Ishmael must be separated from Isaac in this way, but He promises that Ishmael will not suffer (21.8–21).

Finally, Abraham makes a convenant with a Canaanite tribe and plants a tree to show that the Chosen People have begun to occupy their Chosen Land (21.22–34).

INTERPRETATION

In these two chapters there are more stories of wickedness. Abraham lets his wife become the wife of another king (20.2); Sarah drives Hagar and Ishmael into the desert (21.10–14). But again we see how

God was proceeding with His plan of raising up a chosen people. He protects Abraham (Gen. 20), and gives him a son, the first of his 'descendants' (21.1–7). This son must be separated from others, although those 'others' are still under God's care (21.8–21).

NOTES

20.2. Abraham said of Sarah his wife, 'She is my sister': We have already read a story in which Abraham did the same thing (12.10–19). Gen. 12 is written by the Older Writer; Gen. 20 is by the Northern Writer. So perhaps they are two accounts of the same event.

In Gen. 26 there is an account of Isaac telling the same sort of lie, and some people think that this is a third account of the same story.

Whether this took place once or twice or three times, the writers have recorded this event for one reason: to show that God protects His servants even when they are among strangers. (Many students working in foreign countries are strengthened when they remember this truth.)

20.5. In the . . . innocence of my hands I have done this: This story shows that the editors looked on adultery as a sin against God, not only as a sin against another person. The faithfulness of a man and his wife to each other was regarded as a duty to God, as well as a duty to one another.

According to this story, the heathen Abimelech treated women better than Abraham did. In 20.9–11 we read that Abimelech says so to Abraham. (No adultery was committed.)

21.2. Sarah conceived, and bore Abraham a son: This son was Isaac.

1. He was the one who had been promised by God long ago.

2. His coming gave joy, as his name shows: the name Isaac means 'laughter'.

3. He was the first to be born of all the Chosen People of God, who descended from Abraham.

4. He was called 'your son, your only son whom you love' (22.2).

Christian readers may be reminded of Jesus Christ Himself as they read such things about Isaac. What is the explanation?

(a) the writers were not here predicting the birth of Jesus, although we can see many of the statements above are true about Jesus. (No writer in the Bible says that these words are a prediction.)

(b) But Jesus Himself seems to have regarded the joy which they had when Isaac was born as a sign or picture of His own birth (John 8.56).

21.13. I will make a nation of the son of the slave-woman: We have already seen in this story: (a) Sarah's cruelty in driving away Hagar and her son Ishmael, and (b) God's decision that Ishmael must be separated from Isaac, because Isaac is the 'chosen one'. 'Through Isaac your descendants shall be named' (see 21.12b).

But this verse shows us the very important truth, that God loves and cares for Ishmael, and promises to look after him and his people. But He does not love them more than He loves all His human beings. God has a special covenant with His Church today, and there is special work for the Church to do for Him. But God does not love and care for church members more than He cares for those who are not Church members.

Questions on Gen. 20 and 21

Content:

1. Which two people were saved after being sent into the wilderness?

2. What lesson can we learn from their being saved?

Bible:

3. In these last chapters we have read of many disasters, with people suffering. Many people ask, 'Are all disasters sent by God to punish sinners?' What answers can we find in Luke 13.1–5 and John 9.1–3?

Application:

4. In what way was the birth of Isaac different from the births of our own children in the twentieth century?

5. Abimelech, called the 'heathen', behaved better than Abraham towards women. (See 20.9–11.) What explanation do you give when non-Christians behave better than Christians?

6. 'Adultery . . . a sin against God, not only against another person' (p. 99). Explain this.

22
Abraham and Isaac

OUTLINE

22.1–8: Abraham and Sarah had at last been given a son, Isaac, but now Abraham hears God telling him to sacrifice him. He trusts God and obeys Him, and takes Isaac to the place of sacrifice. When Isaac asks where the animal for sacrifice is, Abraham says that God will provide it.

22.9–14: At the moment when Abraham is about to kill Isaac he hears God telling him to stop. Then he sees that a ram is nearby, and he sacrifices the ram instead.

22.15–24: God again promises that Abraham's descendants will be greatly used by Him.

INTERPRETATION

In past times many tribes offered children as sacrifices to their gods. They believed that the gods would not bless them or their crops unless they sacrificed some very valuable thing. Some Israelites believed this. See Judg. 11.29–40 (Jephthah's daughter) and 2 Kings 16.3. Children are still sacrificed today in some places.

But the story is told us because it contains two great truths: the first is that *God Himself provides an offering*; the second is that *God wants us to obey Him willingly*.

1. GOD PROVIDES

Abraham said that God would provide a sacrifice (22.8), but he did not know how God could do it. Then he finds that God has provided (22.13). This part of the story was so important that people later called the place of sacrifice 'God will provide'.

This is what the Israelites found to be true as God led them through the wilderness, and later as He rescued them from the Exile in Babylon. Over and over again they could not see how God could rescue them, but He did provide a way each time. The writer knew that God does this.

The writers were not here predicting the cross of Christ, but Christians are right to see God's action in this story as a way of understanding the cross. We must not say that Jesus was loving and that God was angry, and that Jesus had to 'appease' or 'propitiate' God by dying as a 'lamb'. 'God Himself was *in* Christ reconciling the world to Himself' (2 Cor. 5.19). See also Rom. 8.32: God 'provided'.

"He believed that God was asking him to give up the most precious thing he had" (p. 103).

Four of the eight men who regularly manned this lifeboat gave up their lives when the boat capsized in heavy seas on its way to rescue the crew of a ship in trouble.

2. GOD WANTS US TO HAVE ABRAHAM'S WILLING TRUST

He trusted God although it seemed that God's command to sacrifice Isaac was the opposite of the promise which He had made earlier (as we read in 21.12). According to that promise Isaac was to be the first of Abraham's descendants. He trusted God although he believed that God was asking him to give up the most precious thing he had.

Being a Christian does not mean 'imitating Abraham'. But we are told that if we do have this sort of trust in God we shall be strong enough to stand firm in this world (Heb. 11. 17–19 and 12. 1–2). Faith and trust for a Christian are 'the power to give ourselves up to God'. 'Teach us, good Lord . . . to give and not to count the cost' (from the prayer of St Ignatius Loyola). See also Luke 14.26.

Note: The writer of Heb. 11.19 said that Abraham had such trust that he believed that God would make Isaac alive again after he had been killed. But the writers of Gen. 22 did not say this.

NOTES

22.1a. God tested Abraham: The writers seem to have interpreted these words in the following way: 'God wanted to see if Abraham had enough faith and obedience to be the leader of His Chosen People. So He pretended that He required a sacrifice. Secondly, God wanted to increase Abraham's faith by making him use it. He did not want him to sacrifice Isaac, but He allowed Abraham to think that He wanted a sacrifice (so that his faith should develop).' See Additional Note, Sacrifice, p. 160.

But since the coming of Jesus we can see that God does not treat us like this. We read in James 1.13 that 'God . . . tempts no one'. Good parents do not test their young children's trustfulness or develop their courage by pretending that they are telling them to jump into a deep river. There are plenty of opportunities in family life by which parents can discover how trusting their children are, and can help them to become more trusting. They do not have to set traps or tests or examinations, nor does God have to set special tests for us.

22.1b. God . . . said to Abraham: Again we are told that God 'spoke', as if He were one man talking to another man, or as if Abraham heard a voice like the voice of a radio announcer. But if we can see behind the word 'said', we know that it really means, 'Abraham believed that it was right, he believed that it was the wish of God that he should do this.' Abraham did not want to serve God in any less costly way than those people whom he saw sacrificing their children to the gods they worshipped.

Questions on Gen. 22

Content:

1. 'God said to him' (Gen. 22.1). What does it mean to say that God 'spoke' to Abraham?

2. Why did some people sacrifice their children to their gods (as some still do)?

3. What question did Isaac ask his father?

4. What was the place of sacrifice called afterwards?

5. (a) In what way does this story help us to understand the cross of Christ?

(b) What help do we get from 2 Cor. 5.19 and Rom. 8.32?

Bible:

6. What teaching do we find in this chapter and also in Luke 14.26, 27, 33; and Heb. 11.17–19 and 12.1?

Application:

7. What is the most important lesson which you gain from reading Gen. 22?

8. Abraham discovered that God does not want human sacrifices.

(a) What is the difference, if any, between such sacrifices, and a country sacrificing its young men by sending them to war?

(b) Describe any common practice in the world today which seems to you as terrible as child-sacrifice, and which you believe God is calling people to give up.

(c) How do we know when God is calling us to give up a common practice?

9. Writers on Gen. 22 often quote John 1.36 and call Jesus the 'Lamb' sacrificed on our behalf.

What are the (i) advantages (ii) disadvantages of using the word 'lamb' today when referring to Jesus?

10. A church member said, 'This story shows that if you trust God enough everything will go right for you.' What is your opinion?

23.1—25.18
Abraham's Wisdom, and his Death

OUTLINE

Gen. 23: Sarah dies at Hebron, and Abraham buys land from the Canaanite people of that district in which to bury her. (It was bought and sold with the same customary sentences and the same skill with which Arabs today still buy and sell.)

Gen. 24: Abraham now plans to find a wife for Isaac. He sends a servant to find one who will be of the same religion as Isaac. He also says that, if a wife can be found, she must come and live in Canaan. The servant finds one, Rebekah, whose father and brother allow her to come and to marry Isaac. 'And she became his wife and he loved her.'

25.1–18: Now Abraham marries another wife and, after some years, he dies. We are given names of his descendants. (Each name is the name of a tribe in southern Canaan or northern Arabia.)

INTERPRETATION

Many readers enjoy these ancient stories so much, especially Gen. 24, that they sometimes overlook the message which they contain. The message is that God chose to do His work through a Chosen People. So the buying of a field is more than buying a place for a grave. This is the first time that one of God's Chosen People has owned a piece of the Chosen Land. And Abraham's finding of a wife for Isaac is more than a wise father helping a weak son: he was preparing for future descendants, i.e. by whom there will be a Chosen People. The wife must come and live in Canaan (24.6) because it is the land that God has chosen for His People. In Gen. 24 especially we are shown that these events are according to God's purpose. The servant is careful to consult God as he makes his journey and as he looks for a wife for Isaac (24. 21, 26, 27, 40, 42, 48, 50, 56).

Note: Afterwards Rebekah was not a good wife to Isaac (Gen. 27). But in spite of this Isaac was doing God's will when he married her. In the long story of God's Chosen People there have been many people who were truly chosen by God even though at one time or another they failed Him. This is true of those living before Christ and it is also true of Christians today.

NOTES

23.4. I am a stranger . . . give me property: Abraham had great possessions, but he was still an immigrant in a foreign country (like many millions of people today). His home land was far away. This is the reason why he needed to obtain land in Canaan.

24.4. Take a wife for my son Isaac: Isaac was not a great leader as his father Abraham was. His mother was very old when he was born, and he seems to have been kept at home. He followed his parents' advice rather than make his own way. His father obtained a wife for him.

Yet writers in the Bible repeatedly use the words, 'God is the God of Abraham *and of Isaac* and of Jacob', e.g. in Exodus 3.6. This shows that God does indeed use such a person as Isaac. Christians who are followers are as important to Him as those who are leaders in the Church. Each one counts for one, no one counts for more than one.

24.7. He will send His angel: That is, God will guide you. See Additional Note, Angel, p. 153.

24.12. O Lord . . . grant me success today: This is part of the prayer which Abraham's servant prayed to God. The words remind us of three truths which Jesus afterwards showed us:

1. God is interested in the affairs of our lives, e.g. the woman or man we want to marry, the child we want to have, the job we want to obtain, the examinations we want to pass.

2. He has a purpose for us concerning these things: we are not ruled by fate or by chance.

3. He wants us to pray to Him, to speak to Him of these things, and to discover His purpose (Matt. 7.7).

24.14. By this I shall know: The servant was saying to God, 'Give me a sign. Make the woman who shall be Isaac's wife speak certain words, so that I shall know which one she is.' Readers interpret these words in different ways:

1. Some say that the servant was simply asking for God's guidance as he looked for the right wife for Isaac. A woman who answered courteously, 'Drink, and I will water your camels' would be the right *sort* of wife.

2. Others says that he was asking God to send a magical sign to show which particular woman He intended Isaac to marry.

People often look for this sort of 'sign' by looking for unusual sights or events. In some parts of the world if people see a black bird on their left hand as they set out on a journey they will turn back, and travel another day. They think the bird is a 'sign' of evil. But this is not the way in which God gives His guidance. He gives it as we use the intelligence He has given us, as we listen to the advice of good friends, and especially as we keep in fellowship with Him by regular prayer and by the study of the Bible.

24.58. 'Will you go with this man?' They were not asking Rebekah if she wanted to marry Isaac: they were only asking whether she could leave immediately or would go after ten days. Her father and brother had already decided to send her (24.51).

People ask if Gen. 24 can give help to present-day Christians concerning marriage. The answer is, Yes, because the servant asked God for guidance at every stage of his journey. But some of the customs of which we read here are the customs of those days, rather than the will of God for Christians today. See note on 16.3.

25.8. Abraham ... died in a good old age: He seems to have accepted death as the completion of a long life, not as something to be feared.

In those days Israelites did not believe that they could have any life after death in which there was fellowship with God. See Ps. 88.4, 5. 'Gathered to his people' meant 'went to the place where his ancestors had gone'. But when Jesus came, He taught that God had prepared a life of fellowship with God after his death: 'God said, "I am the God of Abraham. . . ." ' He is not the God of the dead but of the living' (Mark 12.27): i.e. 'Those who have the Lord as their God are not dead. They are living.'

They buried him at Machpelah in Hebron, the place which Jews, Christians and Muslims all regard as the burial place of their 'father'.

Questions on 23.1—25.18

Content:

1. Why did the editors give us this story of Abraham buying land?

2. Isaac was not a great leader like Abraham. Why do writers in the Bible join his name with the names of Abraham and Jacob, e.g. in Mark 12.26–7?

3. What is being referred to in all the following passages: Gen. 24.21, 26, 27, 40, 42, 48, 50, 56?

Bible:

4. In Gen. 24.51 and Matt. 10.4 we read that God chose two people for special work. But both of them later failed to obey Him. Did God *not* choose them? Or did God make a mistake in choosing them? Or is there another answer?

Application:

5. The servant in Gen. 24 asked God for a sign to show him who should be Isaac's wife.

(a) How do non-Christians whom you know look for guidance when they have an important decision to take?

(b) How should Christians obtain guidance? Give a recent example, if possible.

6. Compare the marriage customs of which we read in Gen. 24 with the customs among Christians whom you know.

25.19–34
The Cunning of Jacob

OUTLINE

25.19–26: Isaac and Rebekah have been married for twenty years, and they still have no children. Then, after Isaac has prayed, God gives children to Rebekah. She gives birth to twins of whom Esau comes first and Jacob afterwards. (We seem to see the character of Jacob even in the womb; he appears to be striving to be first.)

25.27–34: When they grow up, Esau becomes a hunter and is often away from home. Jacob becomes a shepherd and lives a more settled life. One day Esau returns home starving, and asks for some of the soup which Jacob is cooking. Jacob sees a way by which he can become the head of the family when Isaac dies. He says, 'I will give you some soup if you will give me your position as the eldest son.' Esau, weak from hunger, agrees to this. So he is given his soup of red lentils, and Jacob claims his position as the 'first son'.

INTERPRETATION

1. GOD'S WORK

In this story readers may think chiefly of what Jacob and Esau did. But the Israelite editors are pointing to what God was doing. 'The parents were childless,' they tell us, 'but God gave them children so that our nation, the Chosen People, could survive.'

2. JACOB AND ESAU

We consider Jacob's behaviour in the note on 25.31, and Esau's in the note on 25.33b. But the writers did not refer to the guilt or innocence of Jacob or Esau. Probably they took the side of Jacob because through him their nation had come into being.

NOTES

25.22b. She went to inquire of the Lord: Rebekah was pregnant with twins, and they were causing her so much trouble that she went to find out if she was going to die. She went to the sort of priest whom we should now call a 'diviner' or 'medium'. Some Israelites believed that he could foretell the future partly through magic. The Israelites made use of such people (see Isa. 8.19) until they found that they could discover God's will through prayer and by using their intelligence, rather than through magic.

The message Rebekah received was that she would live and give birth to 'two nations'. Esau was regarded as the ancestor of the nation of Edom, and Jacob as the ancestor of the nation of Israel. Edomites were the enemies of the Jews during the whole time of which we read in the Old Testament, just as Esau had been the enemy of Jacob for much of their lives.

25.31. First sell me your birthright: Readers today call Jacob cunning and cruel. He waited until Esau was weak with hunger, and then persuaded him to give up his position as head of the family (which was his birthright). Jacob was like a man who visits a sick old woman and then makes her give him all her possessions.

25.33b. He sold his birthright to Jacob: In the Bible there are three interpretations of Esau's act:

(a) The editor of these verses (and Heb. 12.16) says 'he despised his birthright' (25.34).

(b) Malachi 1.1–3 disapproves of Esau, and says that God will always hate the Edomites (descended from Esau) but love the Israelites (descended from Jacob).

(c) St Paul (Rom. 9.9–13) quotes Malachi and adds that God made Jacob to be the stronger while the twins were in their mother's womb. See 25.23. Readers may ask, 'If so, then was Esau really free to resist Jacob?'

There seems to be one lesson in the minds of the above writers, namely: 'Esau avoided responsibility which he should have accepted. He should have been the leader of the "Chosen People". God gives to everyone some responsibility. By accepting it they serve Him. If they abandon it, they sin against God.'

Some Christians have used Esau's conduct as a picture of another temptation that comes to us. This is the temptation to give up a great blessing which will be ours in the future, in exchange for a small blessing which we can get now. Esau gave up the leadership of his family in exchange for lentil soup 'immediately'. See note on 26.2.

Questions on 25.19–34

Content:

1. What work did Esau and Jacob each do?

2. Why did Esau ask Jacob for food and drink?

3. 'Jacob . . . cunning and cruel' (p. 109). Why did the editors critize Esau and not Jacob?

Bible:

4. (a) What practice is referred to in 25.22b and Isa. 8.19?

(b) Why did Israelite leaders forbid this practice later on?

Application:

5. (a) To what extent was Esau free to accept or reject Jacob's invitation to 'sell' (25.31)?

(b) What is your opinion of Paul's statement that God 'chose' Jacob in the womb to be the stronger of the twins?

(c) If things happen to us when we are very young, how free are we to take decisions in later life?

6. 'God gives to everyone some responsibility' (p. 109).

(a) Give examples of people accepting responsibility (i) at work (ii) in a family (iii) in a church congregation.

(b) What happens if they do not accept that responsibility?

(c) What could help such people to accept responsibility?

26.1—28.9
The Theft of Isaac's Blessing

OUTLINE

Gen. 26: The first part of this passage describes Isaac's life in Gerar, in the south of Palestine. He had gone there with his family because there was famine in the north. The story that follows is almost the same as the two stories about Abraham in Gen. 12.10–19 and Gen. 20. When Isaac arrives in Gerar, he is afraid that the people of the district may kill him in order to take his wife Rebekah. So he says that she is his sister. Later he becomes a very successful farmer, and lives peacefully with the neighbouring people. During this time, he receives a promise of blessing from God.

27.1—28.9: The second part tells of the blessing which Isaac gives. His wish is to give his blessing to his elder son, Esau. But Rebekah wants her son, Jacob, to receive it, and she shows Jacob how he can obtain it by a trick. Jacob does what she says. When Esau comes to be blessed, he finds that it is too late. Jacob has to run away from Esau. But, before he goes, Isaac blesses him again.

INTERPRETATION

As in previous chapters, the editors of this story have a single message, namely: 'Nothing can spoil God's plan to raise up a Chosen People, through whom He will save humanity.' They do not make any judgement whether Jacob's actions were 'right' or 'wrong'.

NOTES

26.2. Do not go down to Egypt: There was famine and Isaac expected to go to Egypt where there was food. But God told him not to go, because he would find even better things if he waited (26.3, 4). He trusted God, as Abraham had (see Heb. 11.9), and did not go.

26.7. When the men . . . asked him about his wife, he said, 'She is my sister': This is the third story of this kind in the Book of Genesis. In 12.10–19 we read of Abraham calling Sarah his 'sister' in order to save his own life.

We note, as Abimelech did, that Isaac told a lie. It could have resulted in his wife's becoming the wife of another man, and in a serious quarrel between the two tribes. Some readers may want to follow this up by asking: 'When, if ever, is it right to tell a lie?' e.g. 'Should I lie to save a dying person from great pain of mind? Or when an enemy government is in control of my country?'

27.7. Bring me . . . food . . . that I may bless you: We read of 'blessing' in 26.3–5; 26.24; 27.1–45; 28.1–4. We read of 'cursing' in 27.12, 13, 29.

This story shows that the people of those times held certain ideas about blessings and cursings which do not agree with the teaching of Jesus.

1. They thought that when people gave a blessing, it was always God's power that they were giving.

A person can indeed give a blessing which results in someone receiving God's power. This can happen, for instance, when we pray for someone else.

But a blessing may not have this result at all. God Himself responds to our words of blessing, and He may not respond if our prayer is against His will.

2. They thought that the power given by a blessing was power to become richer and more able to dominate other nations. See 17.20. Later, as they understood more of God's ways, they saw that the result of His blessing was to become wiser and more just. See 1 Kings 3.5–9. Finally, Jesus showed that the result of God's blessing was the 'happiness' of being in a right relationship with God and with other people. See Matt. 5.3–12.

3. They thought that as soon as someone spoke words of blessing on another person, the power passed into that person: it could not be stopped (27.33, 35). In the same way they believed that when people were cursed they could not escape the evil that was put upon them. They believed that there was power in the words themselves, i.e. that the words had 'magic'.

We may notice two things about the teaching of Jesus:

(a) Jesus taught that a man's own sinfulness harms him more than any evil coming from outside. 'The things which come out of a man are what defile him' (Mark 7.15; and Mark 7.16–23).

(b) Even those who believe that power to bring evil exists in the actual words of a curse can find out that God's power and love are greater. God is able to protect those who trust Him, and He does so (Rom. 8.38, 39).

27.19. Jacob said to his father, 'I am Esau': The writers of Genesis do not criticize the deceit of Rebekah and Jacob. They regarded their action as skill, not as wrongdoing. Jacob was at first unwilling to deceive Isaac, *not* because it was wrong, but because he might be found out (27.12). There seemed to him to be nothing wrong in using the Name of God to support his lie (27.20). Only later God's People learnt that such deceit is against His will.

28.1. Isaac ... charged him, 'You shall not marry one of the Canaanite women': From which people can a man choose his wife, or a wife choose her husband?

Isaac and Rebekah helped Jacob to choose a wife from his own tribe and religion, and not from the Canaanites. According to 29.8 Jacob married his own cousins, who were, of course, of his own religion.

But according to 26.34 Esau had chosen wives from a different tribe, the Hittites.

At the time when Isaac lived, and at the time when the Older Writer (who tells us that Esau married heathens) was writing, the Israelites had no law which forbade them to marry non-Israelites. But much later they regarded it as a serious sin to do so. The Priestly Writer (who wrote 28.6–9) lived at a time when they regarded it as a sin.

Does this have any message for Christians and for these days? There is no rule which tells Christians who are the people from whom they may choose their future wives or husbands. But there is some guidance for us, e.g.:

1. Christians need to think very seriously before marrying.

2. When a man and a woman plan to get married, they are planning to join two families. Their plan, therefore, concerns their relatives as well as themselves. Isaac certainly believed this (28.1, 2).

3. We are free to marry someone from another tribe or race. But if there is misunderstanding or enmity between the tribes or races, those who marry may find added difficulties. They need to recognize these difficulties before the marriage takes place.

Questions on 26.1—28.9

Words:

1. (a) Read the note on 27.7, the Additional Note, Blessing, on p. 154, and the following passages: 26.24, 27.27–9, 28.14. Say in each case what the one who received the blessing expected to result from it.

(b) In what way do the following verses show what God gives by His blessing? 1 Kings 3.5–9; Matt. 5.3–12; Eph. 1.3, 4

Content:

2. To whom did Isaac want to give his blessing?

3. Why did the editors of Genesis include this story of deceitfulness?

Bible:

4. Jesus compared Nathaniel to Jacob (John 1.45–51). What was the chief difference between those two men?

5. 'Cursings' are mentioned in these chapters. What truth about cursing can we discover from Mark 7.15, and Rom. 8.38, 39?

Application:

6. 'Jacob was at first unwilling to deceive Isaac, *not* because it was wrong, but because he might be found out' (p. 112). A modern writer says that the only commandment most people take seriously is: 'Thou shalt not be found out.' How far do you agree or disagree with him? Give examples from everyday life.

---

7. What is your answer to the question on p. 111: 'When, if ever, is it right to tell a lie?'

8. It is not clear whether Esau married someone from a different tribe and religion ('mixed marriage').

(a) What has been the ancient custom about mixed marriages in your Church, and what was the reason for that custom?

(b) What regulation, if any, does your Church have concerning the marriage of a Christian with a non-Christian, or with a member of another Christian denomination?

(c) Give examples from everyday life to show (i) the advantages and (ii) the disadvantages of mixed marriages.

28.10–22
God's Summons to Jacob

OUTLINE

28.10–22: The events which are described here took place as Jacob was escaping from the anger of Esau.

28.11–15: Jacob falls asleep, and in a dream sees angels coming to protect him. He dreams that God is speaking to him and promising to give him land, to take care of him, and to help him to return home.

28.16, 17: Jacob wakes up, and sees that he has gone to sleep in a place in which people usually worship, and is greatly afraid.

28.18–22: But he wants to make some answer to God's message, so he does two things. First he makes the stone which he had used for a pillow into a sacred stone by pouring oil on it. Then he tells God that he will serve Him faithfully if God will give him the things that he most wants.

INTERPRETATION

This event is the first part of the training which God gave Jacob. His training is the important part of these verses. But Jacob needed very many years of correction and guidance. This is clear from the way in which he tried to bargain with God, and from his doubts about God's promises. His words in 28.20–2 mean, 'I will serve you only on condition that you give me everything I want.'

But he made a beginning, i.e. it was the first time that Jacob understood that God was calling him. He was like a lump of wet clay

114

that needs to be made into a shape by the potter's hands before it can be used. In this dream he saw that God was wanting to take him up into His hands to mould him. He saw that the times of temptation and suffering (Gen. 29—35) could be times when God was shaping and training him. In the end Jacob did become a person of whom God made great use.

NOTES

28.11. Jacob . . . came to a certain place: The place where Jacob slept was probably a Canaanite (pagan) place of worship, that is to say, it was not a place kept for the worship of Yahweh only. This is not surprising. The religion of the Israelites was not at that time totally separate from the religious practices of pagans. Indeed, Israelites continued for many hundreds of years to worship Yahweh at the stones of Bethel which the pagan Canaanites held as sacred. But later, e.g. in Hosea's time, the prophets saw that this custom was preventing them from giving their full loyalty to Yahweh. See Hos. 4.12, 13.

Words which show that this place was a pagan temple are:

Ladder (28.12): Jacob probably saw a ladder of 'steps' in his dream because he had gone to sleep near the stone steps leading to the old pagan temple.

Pillar (28.18): He made his stone pillow into a pillar or *massebah*. A *massebah* was a stone which pagans used in order to show that God was present. At that time the Israelites also used it in this way. It thus became sacred. Jacob set it aside for this purpose by pouring oil on it.

Luz (28.19): This was the Canaanite name for the place: afterwards it was called Bethel.

28.12a. He dreamed: We may ask 'Did God send this dream, or was it only the imagination of Jacob?' Various answers to this question will be given by different Christians, but here is one answer:

This dream, and other dreams, can indeed be described as gifts from God, and for the following reason: it is God who has given us our minds. A mind works in the way that God has planned. It has some thoughts which we know about and some which are hidden from us. Two kinds of thoughts which the mind often hides away are those things about which we are ashamed, and those things about which we are afraid. But such things should not remain hidden: we cannot confess a sin or face a fearful thing with courage if they are hidden from us. How can they be shown to us? A dream is one way, because in a dream our minds often show these hidden things to us. We cannot see them clearly, because they come to us in the form of a picture. But we can sometimes interpret the picture, as the following story shows.

St Peter had a dream in which he refused to eat animals that Jews called 'unclean'; but he was told that he ought to eat them (Acts 10.9–16). When he woke up he saw that this was a picture of his own feelings. The dream showed him that he had feelings of shame and guilt because he was unwilling to eat with non-Jews. Because of the dream he changed his outlook towards the non-Jews who came to see him just afterwards. We can say that God wanted St Peter to change his outlook towards non-Jews, but He did not force him to do so. He provided St Peter with a mind, and the mind gave St Peter a dream. St Peter was able to interpret the dream because he took notice of other events which occurred at that time. Through his interpretation he discovered what God wanted him to do. Then he did it.

28.12b. There was a ladder set up on the earth: When Jacob saw this in his dream, he interpreted it as showing that God is not separated from human beings (28.16). The 'steps' remind people that communion between God and ourselves is possible.

Perhaps this part of his dream showed him another truth, namely, that God is present with us even when we are away from places where we have been accustomed to know His presence, e.g. our homes and our places of worship. We remember that Jacob was far from his home at this place.

28.16. The Lord is in this place, and I did not know it: Jacob was away from his home, and thought that he could only find God in his home town. He was astonished that God was present and revealed Himself in a foreign country.

When the Jews were taken into exile in Babylon many years later, they also were surprised when Ezekiel taught them that God was with them in exile (Ezek. 11.16; 34.12). So today some students studying in a foreign country feel that they have left God at home, and are surprised to find that He is with them, even in a country where few people seem to believe in God.

28.17. How awesome is this place: Jacob felt 'awe' in God's presence. Being full of 'awe' is not being terrified, but having reverence and deep respect for God, feeling that He is 'holy', 'mysterious', 'different'. There are many parts in an act of worship, but unless there is awe and wonder, the worship is seriously lacking. See Isa. 6.1–5; Rev. 4.9–11.

Questions on 28.10–22

Words:

1. The Hebrew word *yare* is translated 'awesome' in 28.17.

(a) How is it translated in this verse in other languages and translations which you know?

(b) How is it translated in Lev. 19.30?

Content:

2. Why did Jacob run away from home?

3. (a) What did Jacob learn from his dream?

(b) What two things did he do after having the dream?

Bible:

4. What is the chief difference between the vow made by Jacob (Gen. 28.20–2) and the prayer of Jesus recorded in Mark 14.36?

5. In what way is the teaching of Gen. 28.16 like the teaching of (a) Luke 24.30–2; (b) John 6.36?

Application:

6. 'Unless there is awe and wonder the worship is seriously lacking' (p. 116).

(a) What is your opinion?

(b) If you are a member of a Church, describe a time when there was 'awe' in the service.

(c) What helps us to feel 'awe', and what hinders us from it?

7. (a) Jacob had a 'dream'. What connection is there between his dream and St Peter's dream (Acts 10.9–16)?

(b) One person says that it is so difficult to interpret dreams that we should forget them or laugh at them. Another person says, 'Dreams show me feelings of my own which had been hidden from me. I think God wants me to take them seriously.' What do you think? Give reasons.

29.1—32.2
God's Preparation of Jacob

OUTLINE

This is the story of the twenty years that Jacob spent with his uncle, Laban.
29.1–14: Jacob reaches Haran after a journey of about three hundred miles. Very soon he meets his cousin Rachel, and immediately wants to marry her.
29.15–20: Rachel's father, Laban, agrees that Jacob can marry her if he works for him for seven years without payment. Jacob does this. (He probably hoped that he would become Laban's heir, for Laban had no sons.)
29.21–30: When it is time for Jacob to marry Rachel, Laban tricks him by dressing his older daughter, Leah, in the wedding clothes. So Jacob finds afterwards that he has married Leah instead of Rachel. He is told by Laban that he can marry Rachel after one week if he promises to work for him for seven years more. Jacob makes his promise, and in the end marries Rachel.
29.31—30.24: Leah and her slave girl and Rachel's slave girl give Jacob ten sons and a daughter. After a long time Rachel too has a son, Joseph. These eleven sons are regarded as the ancestors of eleven tribes of Israel. (The twelfth son, Benjamin, was born much later.)
30.25—31.21: Jacob now wishes to go home, but Laban does not want him to, because Jacob is a skilled shepherd. Jacob agrees to stay if Laban will give him all the sheep which are not completely white and all the goats which are not completely black. Laban agrees. Laban and Jacob each do their best to deceive the other, but Jacob is the more cunning of the two. He makes the animals which are partly black and partly white breed far more than the others. Finally he tricks Laban by going away with his wives and children and possessions while Laban is absent from home.
31.22–55: Laban follows after Jacob. He is angry because Jacob has tricked him, and because he thinks Jacob has stolen his family's 'image' (Rachel was really the thief). But Jacob says that God Himself had told them to go home; and Laban agrees, because he has had a dream in which God spoke to him. Laban and Jacob make an agreement or 'covenant', and they separate from each other in peace.
32.1, 2: As Jacob goes away, something happens to him which he calls 'a meeting with God's angels'.
Note: In 29.1—32.2 the editors have used the writings of the Older Writer and of the Northern Writer and of the Priestly Writer. This would explain why some stories are told twice over and in different

ways. For example, the Northern Writer gives one sign of the agreement between Laban and Jacob (31.50), the Older Writer gives a different sign (31.52).

INTERPRETATION

Some of those who handed down this story by word of mouth must have done so chiefly because they enjoyed the story of two cunning men, Laban and Jacob, each trying to deceive the other. And we too can read it in that way.

Others probably told the story because it shows how Jacob (the ancestor of the people of Israel) got the better of Laban (who is thought of as the ancestor of the Aramaeans, the people of Syria). Others told it because it gave the reason why there was a boundary between Israel and the country of Syria (31.48).

But, as we have seen in our study of previous chapters, the editors' aim was to show how God was preparing Jacob to be the leader of the Chosen People. Jacob suffered during this time, partly because he treated Esau so badly. But God was looking after him, and Jacob knew this. See 31.42.

NOTES

29.16. The older was Leah: At first Leah seems a person whom we should pity: she had weak eyes, and she became the wife of Jacob against his wishes; Jacob did not love her as he loved Rachel. But she became the mother of Judah, who was the ancestor of David; and Jesus was called 'son of David' (Matt. 1.1).

29.19. I give her to you: Laban seems to have given Rachel to Jacob without asking her if she was willing. Later he gave Leah to him in the same way. He regarded the women as his property, to be used as he decided. We also see that Jacob took a second wife only one week after he had married Leah. And he not only had two wives; he had children by two slave-girls also.

This was the way in which marriages were carried out at that time, and are still being carried out in some places. (Some of those customs are necessary, e.g. where parents *have to* find marriage partners for their children.) How should we regard those Old Testament customs?

1. By avoiding any condemnation, realizing that they lived before the Ten Commandments had been given, and long before Christ showed the way to live.

2. By making sure that we follow better customs today. For example: (a) in preparing men and women for marriage; (b) in giving women their rightful position in society and in marriage.

"Giving women their rightful position in society" (p. 119).

What is their right position? Is it working at home and looking after the children (see upper picture from Thailand) or earning money in the office (see lower picture from London)? Should women combine the two?

30.38. He set the rods which he had peeled in front of the flocks:
Laban told Jacob that he could take all the sheep and goats which were
partly black and partly white, and Jacob increased the number of these
animals with great success. We do not know how he did it. This
passage says that he did it by making the pregnant animals look at
sticks which were partly dark in colour and partly white. Perhaps in
those days people believed that this would cause the young to be born
partly black and partly white. Today we think there was some other
reason. Perhaps Jacob put the black-and-white rams with the herd and
kept the other rams apart. In this way the herd would be likely to
produce many black-and-white young. (See 31.12.) But if we think this
is what happened, it need not cause us to distrust the writers of this
passage. They did not write it in order to give us a textbook of animal
breeding, but to show how God works with someone who is His
servant, even though that servant has used his free will to be dishonest.

31.19. Rachel stole her father's household gods: These gods were
called *teraphim*. They were images which people used magically,
hoping in this way to obtain advice and to communicate with their
ancestors. At that time the Israelites did not think it was wrong for them,
as worshippers of the true God, to use such images. But in the days of the
great prophets, nearly a thousand years later, the Jews learnt that someone who trusts God fully does not need such things (2 Kings 23.24).

Why did Rachel take the *teraphim*? Because she hoped that if Jacob
had them he would become the heir to Laban. It was the custom that the
future head of a family should have the *teraphim*. As we know, her plan
was not successful.

31.36. What is my sin? Jacob here spoke of sin as injuring a fellow
human being. But sin is also breaking our relationship with God
Himself. See Additional Note, Sin, p. 162.

Questions on 29.1—32.2

Content:

1. On what condition did Laban let Jacob marry Rachel?

2. Describe one trick which Laban played on Jacob, and one trick
which Jacob played on Laban.

3. Before they parted, what did Laban and Jacob agree to do?

4. In what way did Jacob suffer? How did he regard his suffering?

Bible:

5. 'What is my sin?' (Gen. 31.36). Read the Additional Note on
Sin, p. 162. Read also (a) 13.13 (b) 31.36 (c) 39.9 and in each case

say which of the following meanings of sin the writer had in mind (i) An offence against God (ii) An offence against another person.

Application:

6. What important lesson do you find in Gen. 29—31?

7. 'Laban regarded the women as his property' (p. 119).

(a) How far has the attitude of men towards women changed since those days?

(b) If it has changed for the better, what further improvement is needed?

32.3–32
Jacob's Turning Point

OUTLINE

32.3–23: As Jacob gets nearer to Canaan he knows that Esau will meet him with 400 men. He is very much afraid. (Twenty years before this he took Esau's 'birthright' (Gen. 27.41).) First he prays to God. Then he sends presents to Esau. Lastly, in the evening, he sends his family across the River Jabbok. Then he is alone in the darkness of the night.
32.24–32: During the night he feels that someone is wrestling with him, and his thigh becomes twisted. This person is called a 'man' in 32.24 and 25, 'God' in 32.28 and 30, but Hosea calls the person 'the angel' (Hos. 12.2–4). Then he holds on to his opponent, and as he does so he asks for a blessing. The blessing which he receives is a new name, Israel (which probably means 'God strives').

INTERPRETATION

1. People handed down this story from one generation to another for hundreds of years before the Older Writer wrote it down. Why did they preserve it?

(a) Some perhaps told it because it seemed to refer to the 'spirits' of their land. For them, the 'man' who met Jacob was the river-spirit. They thought that river-spirits did not like people crossing their river, since those who crossed were showing themselves to be stronger than the river. Even today many people think the same, and when they build bridges they make offerings to the spirit of the river.

(b) Some probably told it because it explained why Jacob was afterwards called Israel (32.27, 28).

(c) Others, because it explained why a place was called Peniel (32.30).

(d) Others, because it explained why there was a Jewish religious law against eating the thigh of an animal (32.32).

2. But the chief aim of the editors of Genesis was to tell a story about God visiting Jacob and changing his life. For us readers the most important truth behind the story is the struggle which Jacob had in his spirit with God. The outward sign of that struggle was the 'twisting of his thigh'. He knew that Esau was coming, and did not feel strong enough to meet him. Then he felt that God was saying, 'You think that you have to depend on your own strength (on your own "thigh"). But hold on to Me, and trust Me.' See 32.26b: 'Jacob held on to the man'. Human beings, throughout the ages, have experienced this sort of struggle, and have in the end and with difficulty put their trust in God rather than in themselves.

Jacob was also learning other truths about God and about himself:

(a) That God is near at hand. He was not approaching God. God was visiting him.

(b) That God makes possible a change in our lives. For Jacob the sign of a change was his new name Israel. He did not become a perfect person, but he was now different. When people turn from their old life and become Christian they do not become immediately saintly. But they are going in the right direction.

NOTES

32.9. Jacob said, 'O God of my father Abraham': We read of Jacob's prayer in 32.9–12. At the beginning of this prayer Jacob seems to be reminding God of His promises. But this is not really so. As Jacob addresses God he reminds himself of the kind of person God is. He says that God has been the Father and protector of Abraham and Isaac; that He has promised to help Jacob to return home; that He is full of 'steadfast love' and 'faithfulness' (32.10).

We must notice these two words since they are used throughout the Bible when a writer is speaking of God. The word *chesed* (here 'steadfast love') is sometimes translated 'mercy' or 'loving-kindness'. The word which is translated 'faithfulness' is sometimes translated 'truth'; God is 'true' because He keeps His promises; He never changes in character. See Additional Note, Steadfast love, p. 163.

Then Jacob admits his own unworthiness.

Lastly he asks for God's protection; he tells God that he is afraid.

32.29. Jacob asked him, 'Tell me, I pray, your name': The 'name' of

God means the character of God as He has revealed it. So these words may mean, 'Make known to me what sort of God You are. Then I can worship You.' So Christians often begin a prayer to God by remembering what sort of God He is. One old prayer begins, 'O God, You are always more ready to hear than we to pray . . .'.

But perhaps Jacob still wanted to make use of God in a magical way. In the Old Testament when people ask the name of strangers they are often trying to get power over them. See Additional Note, Name, p. 158.

Questions on 32.3–32

Words:

1. The Hebrew word *chesed* (32.10) is translated 'steadfast love' in the RSV. Compare this with the translation given in (a) another English version; (b) any other language which you know.

Content:

2. Why was Jacob afraid to meet Esau?

3. What three things did he do because he was afraid?

4. What symbols or signs were there that Jacob had been engaged in a struggle?

5. What was the chief reason that the editors gave us this story?

Bible:

6. Writers use the word 'steadfast love' (*chesed*) to show us something about God. See Additional Note on p. 163. In which *five* of the following passages do we find the same or nearly the same teaching about God? (i) Psalm 51.1 (ii) Psalm 93.1 (iii) Hosea 2.19 (iv) Rom. 5.8 (v) Eph. 2.8 (vi) 1 Tim. 1.12–15 (vii) Rev. 4.11

Application:

7. 'God is near at hand' (p. 123). See also Ps. 139.7–10. In view of this truth

(a) What is the meaning of the words 'God *visited* Jacob'?

(b) What is the meaning of the hymn '*Come* Holy Ghost our souls inspire'?

8. In what way have you (or anyone else of whom you have heard) had an experience somewhat like Jacob's experience recorded in Gen. 32.24–32?

9. Is the receiving of a new name in Baptism like Jacob's receiving of a new name? If so, in what way?

10. Compare the experiences recorded in Gen. 32.24–32 and Gen. 28.10–22.

33.1—37.1
Jacob's Return

OUTLINE

In this passage we read several different stories about Jacob as he returned from Haran to Canaan.

Gen. 33: Jacob crosses the river and meets Esau. He is still very much afraid, but Esau forgives him, and they are at last reunited. Jacob gives Esau half his possessions; and Esau, by accepting this gift, shows that he accepts Jacob himself. Then the two brothers part; Esau goes to Seir, and Jacob goes to Canaan. There he buys land near the town of Shechem.

Gen. 34: The son of the Canaanite chief of that district breaks the tribal law by having sexual intercourse with Jacob's daughter, Dinah. The chief and his son, called Shechem, suggest two ways of settling the matter; either Shechem will pay a fine, or the Israelites will be given permission to marry into that tribe and to use their land. Jacob's sons, Simeon and Levi, decide to trick the tribe. They agree to the second suggestion, but they say that all the men of the tribe must first be circumcised. This is agreed to. Then, just after the circumcision has taken place, and during their time of pain, Simeon and Levi kill all the men of the tribe.

Gen. 35: Jacob now travels towards Hebron where his father, Isaac, is still living. He is told by God to visit Bethel on the way, and he prepares for this visit by making all his followers put away their charms and pagan idols. Then he worships God at Bethel. As they continue their journey Rachel dies as she gives birth to Jacob's twelfth son, Benjamin. When Jacob reaches Hebron, he and Esau are present when their father Isaac dies.

(Gen. 35.9–13 were written by the Priestly Writer. They contain parts of the story which we have already read in Gen. 28.10–22 and Gen. 32.23–32, which were the work of the other writers.)

Gen. 36: Esau and Jacob agree to occupy different parts of the country. A list of Esau's descendants follows.

INTERPRETATION

1. THE STORY OF ESAU AND JACOB (GEN. 33.1–16)

There are two events in Genesis 33 in which the writers are saying to us, 'Look, this is *something which God was doing*: it did not happen by chance.' The first event is the reuniting of the brothers (33.10b). See note below on 33.10. Jacob and Esau are reunited, and it is God who has made this possible.

The other event is Jacob's buying land near Shechem. Again the editors are saying, 'God was guiding Jacob to do this. This was the next step in God's providing a land for His people to occupy.'

2. THE STORY OF DINAH (GEN. 34)

This seems at first to be a story about individual people, Dinah, Simeon, etc. But many people believe that in Genesis 34 we are reading about whole tribes rather than individual people. They tell how descendants of Leah, through her daughter Dinah, became united with a Canaanite tribe, and that later the tribes of Simeon and Levi attacked this tribe by treachery. It was the custom to speak about tribes by using the names of their chiefs or founders. In the same way modern newspapers sometimes say that a prime minister or other leader has said or decided something, when they really mean that the whole government party has done so.

But the interpetation of Gen. 34 remains the same, whether it is about tribes or about individual people:

(a) The story was a *call to be separate*. See 34.14.

(b) It was a *condemnation of treachery*. See 34.30.

NOTES

33.10. To see your face is like seeing the face of God: Probably Jacob was complimenting Esau to prevent him being angry. But when two people have been enemies and are reconciled, they may indeed feel that they are in the presence of God who brought them together.

34.9. Make marriages with us: The chief begged Jacob to unite with his tribe. But Israelites believed that God would not allow this. He could not use them as His People unless they kept themselves faithful to Him. It would be impossible for them to be faithful to God if they united with another tribe, and shared strange customs and strange gods. This is the position in which Christians are today. On the one hand they are told by God to be in the world and associate with everyone; on the other hand, they must remain in some way different in order to remain faithful. A much respected Christian was invited to be chief of a village where nearly all the people were pagan. Should he refuse? As a Christian he would not be able to perform the traditional sacrifices. Or should he accept the invitation in order to lead the people into better ways of living? Part of Jesus' prayer for His followers was: 'I do not pray that thou shouldst take them out of the world, but that thou shouldst keep them from the evil one' (John 17.15).

34.30. You have brought this trouble on me: This is Jacob's very mild rebuke of the treachery of Simeon and Levi. These two sons of Levi had told the chief that his men must be circumcised in order to survive. But after this had been done, they were all killed. This action of Simeon and Levi was a dreadful sin. See Gen. 49.5–7. It did not become a good action because it was committed against non-Israelites. God has never permitted His people to do evil in order that good may result. See Rom. 3.8.

Questions on 33.1—37.1

Content:

1. (a) We read earlier of the separation between Esau and Jacob. Who caused it?

(b) What did Jacob do in order to be reunited with Esau?

(c) In what ways did Esau show his goodwill to Jacob?

2. Why did the editor of Genesis tell us (33.19) that Jacob bought land?

Bible:

3. Show in each of the following pairs how the teaching of the first passage is related to the teaching of the second:

(a) Gen. 34.9 and 10, and John 17.14 and 15;

(b) Gen. 35.2 and Col. 3.8–10.

Application:

4. Read 33.4–10.

(a) What makes reconciliation possible?

(b) What can the people who have caused the trouble do when they are forgiven? Give examples from everyday life.

5. We read in Gen. 34 that Jacob and the Israelites kept apart from the Canaanites.

(a) Is it ever necessary for Christians to refuse to associate with non-Christians? Give examples.

(b) Which temptation is the greater for Christians whom you know: to keep apart from the rest of the community, *or* to be hardly any different from them?

(c) Give an example of Christians fully joining in the life of the local community.

(d) Did Jesus keep Himself apart, or did He associate with others?

6. 'Put away the foreign gods . . . then let us go up to Bethel' (35, 2, 3). In the Christian Baptism service, candidates are told: 'You must affirm your allegiance to Christ and your rejection of all that is evil.' What practices do candidates have to give up in your experience before they can be baptized?

Special Note D:
The Stories about Jacob

We have read about Jacob in Gen. 25.19—37.1. We shall also read of him in the stories about Joseph. As we read about Jacob we saw some of his weaknesses, that he was deceitful, cruel, cowardly and selfish. We saw in Gen. 25 and 27 how he cheated Esau, in Gen. 27 how he deceived his father Isaac, in Gen. 28 how he bargained with God, in Gen. 30 how he tricked Laban. Jesus was thinking of Jacob when He looked at Nathaniel and said, 'Here is an *Israelite* worthy of the name; there is nothing false in him' (John 1.47 NEB); i.e. he is not like Jacob who was called Israel but in whom was much falseness.

We may ask, 'Why did the Jews hold Jacob in honour? Why do the editors of 25.19—37.1 express criticism of Esau but not of Jacob? Why did Jesus Himself join Jacob's name with the name of Abraham in the words, 'The God of Abraham and the God of Isaac and the God of Jacob' (Mark 12.26; compare Exod. 3.6)? But there are answers:

Jacob was held in honour because his name was given to the whole of the Chosen People. His name was changed to 'Israel', and the Jews since that time have been called 'Israel'. Although the letter to the Hebrews calls Abraham 'our father', Jacob was the father of the Twelve Tribes. His sons were the beginning of the 'Twelve Tribes of Israel'.

Another reason why Jacob was honoured is that he overcame Esau. The Jews hated Esau because they regarded him as the ancestor of the Edomites, and there was continual hatred between the Edomites and the Jews for 1,500 years. The Edomites lived by hunting and fighting in the wild hills south of the Dead Sea; the Jews were shepherds and farmers in the rich valleys of Canaan, and despised the Edomites.

Another reason is that Jacob was the sort of person whom the Jews admired in the days of which we read in the Old Testament. They admired someone who was cunning and successful. In those days the Jews were not the only nation to regard a deceitful person as a national hero. The Greeks held cunning Odysseus in great honour. In the fables of many nations cunning animals, not beautiful ones, are praised and successful.

But the main reason why the editors of Genesis do not condemn Jacob is that Jacob, in spite of his great faults, was willing to be trained by God. He could therefore be used by God. This is the reason why Jesus could put Jacob's name alongside the name of Abraham, as we have seen.

'God chooses not only unusually strong people like Abraham: He chooses ordinary ones like Jacob' (p. 131).

As these fishermen haul in their nets on a beach in Malaysia, the less strong as well as the very strong are needed.

From this we are led to the following truths about God:

1. He chooses not only unusually strong people like Abraham. He chooses ordinary ones like Jacob (if they are willing to be trained).

2. He chooses people in spite of their weakness and sin, not because of their goodness. He must have hated Jacob's cruelty and deceit, but He loved Jacob.

If that is true, then we can see what sort of Church God can use to do His work in the world. The Church is a family of ordinary, weak, sinful people, who have been called by God in spite of their weaknesses. We who are its members depend on His grace, and we have no right to make ourselves the judges of people like Jacob. Conflict among Christians shows how sinful we are.

Questions on Special Note D

1. Why did Jesus contrast Jacob and Nathaniel in John 1.47?

2. Why are modern Jews called the people of 'Israel'?

3. What is the chief reason that Jacob has received honour rather than condemnation?

4. Why is it not right for members of the Church to pass judgement on Jacob?

37.2—38.30
Joseph taken to Egypt

OUTLINE

We read here how Joseph's brothers hated him; and how strangers took him to Egypt.

37.2–11: Joseph's brothers hate him, and for many reasons. He is only their half-brother; he tells his father when they behave badly; his father gives him special attention (the robe he gave Joseph was probably the sort which was worn by those who did not do manual work); he has dreams in which he is their head.

37.12–36: Joseph's father sends him to his brothers while they are away from home, and they decide to kill him. We then read two different stories about what happened next. According to the Older Writer, Judah saves Joseph from being killed by persuading the brothers to sell him to the Ishmaelites (37.25–7, 28b). But according to the Northern Writer Reuben saved him, and he was sold to Midianites (37.19–23, 28a). Then the brothers tell Jacob that Joseph is dead.

Gen. 38: The story of Judah's family now follows, but it has nothing to do with the story of Joseph. The Old Writer recorded it because the tribe of Judah became important, and David belonged to it (see Matt. 1.2–6). In this story Judah's eldest son, Er, is married to a Canaanite called Tamar. When Er dies, Judah wants his second son, Onan, to take Tamar as his wife, but Onan refuses. Then Tamar pretends to be a prostitute at a pagan shrine, and Judah finds her there. He does not know who she is, and becomes the father of her children.

INTERPRETATION

The great truth in Genesis 37 is that *God can make use of our sufferings*, but that it is often impossible for us to understand this while the suffering continues.

When Joseph was seventeen his brothers threw him into a pit, and he was taken away into Egypt; and at that time he could probably not think of anything beyond his troubles. But when he was very old, he could look back at these events and see that God used them as a way of saving others. We read in 50.20 that Joseph said to his brother, 'You meant evil against me, but God meant it for good, to bring it about that many people should be kept alive.' These words do not mean that God sent the suffering, but that He used it for the benefit of many people.

NOTES

37.5. Joseph had a dream: We have already seen that it is God's will that we have dreams. It is often His will that we should learn from them (see note on 28.12). But it is very hard indeed to interpret them in the right way. Joseph did not say that the dream showed that God had appointed him to be head over his brothers; nor can we say this. His family, interpreting the dream, thought that Joseph would become their leader, and were angry and afraid. See note on 40.8. (Many people who feel that they are being treated as 'unimportant' have dreams in which they are 'important'. But usually they do not tell the dream to others!)

37.35. I shall go down to Sheol: When Jacob was told that Joseph was dead, he said, 'I shall die also.' Like all Israelites, Jacob believed that after death a person went for ever into a place of dim light called 'Sheol'. There was no fellowship with God there. ('In death there is no remembrance of thee' (Psalm 6.5).) But, much later, some people did hope to reach life after death. See Dan. 12.2. As Christians, we believe that if someone is truly in fellowship with God in this life, that fellowship will not be broken when their body dies. If God has me now, He will not let me go at death. See John 5.24.

37.36. Pharaoh: In Egypt the king was called the Pharaoh. We do not know which Pharaoh was reigning when Joseph was taken to Egypt. Some people think that it was one of the Hyksos-Pharaohs; the Hyksos were Semites who ruled over Egypt from 1700 BC to 1550 BC. Joseph (and the other Israelites) probably came into Egypt in about 1600 BC, i.e. about fifty years before the end of the reign of the Hyksos-Pharaohs. If this is so, it would provide one reason why the Pharaoh gave Joseph his high position: Joseph and he were both Semites. After the Hyksos-Pharaohs ceased to rule, the Israelites became slaves.

38.7. Er . . . was wicked . . . the Lord slew him: This, like 38.10, is an interpretation of the editors that God punished him. Clearly their ideas about God were different from the ideas of Christians. They seem to have regarded every event (such as Er's death) as being directly caused by God Himself. See notes on 6.7a; 19.25.

38.8. Perform the duty of a brother-in-law to her: In these words Judah was telling his son Onan to keep the custom of Levirate marriage. He says, 'You are her husband's brother. Go and make her your wife so that children may be born to her and to our family.' By this custom a woman was saved from the loneliness of being a widow, and she could continue to bear children inside her husband's family. For those and other reasons the custom continues in many parts of the world today. Christian widows need to be looked after by members of the family, even though married brother-in-laws are usually not allowed to marry them. Most Christians do not follow the custom of Levirate marriage because (a) it may not take into account the wishes of the woman, and (b) if her husband's brother is already married she would become the second wife or one of several wives.

Onan refused to help the family by keeping this custom. This is what 38.9 means. In the past readers have sometimes misunderstood this verse and said that Onan was using his sex organs for his private pleasure. But that is not the subject of this verse.

Questions on 37.2—38.30

Words:
1. What did the Jews think of when they used the word 'Sheol'?
Content:
2. What three things made Joseph's brothers hate him?

---

3. Are the following statements 'true' or 'false'? Give reasons for your answers.

(a) God sent suffering to Joseph.

(b) Israelites believed that when they died they would no longer have fellowship with God.

Bible:
4. In what way is the teaching of 1 Cor. 1.26–9 like the teaching of Gen. 37.18 and 50.20?

5. In what way is the teaching of John 13.1 and Phil. 1.23 different from the teaching of Gen. 37.35 and Psalm 6.5?

Application:
6. 'God can make use of our sufferings' (p. 132). Give an example of this from everyday life.

7. The Israelites took care of a widow by making her the wife of her husband's brother.

(a) Do you know of people who have this custom today? If you do, say what are its advantages to the widows.

(b) What is the Church in your country doing for widows and old people?

8. 'It is hard to interpret dreams' (p. 132). What would you reply to a theological student who said, 'I know that God wants me to be a priest because I have twice seen myself dressed in priest's robes in a dream'?

39, 40, 41
Joseph in Prison and Joseph the Ruler

OUTLINE

Gen. 39: Joseph becomes slave to Potiphar, an officer of the Pharaoh, who finds him to be obedient and reliable. Potiphar's wife tries to make him commit adultery with her, but he resists the temptation. Because she cannot persuade him, she brings a false accusation against him, and he is put into prison.

Gen. 40: Joseph interprets the dreams of two Egyptian officials who are in prison. He says that the dreams foretell future events, and later we read that the events took place just as he said.

"He says that dreams foretell future events." (p. 134)

People look for guidance from many sources. A "diviner" in Calcutta and Madame Nicole in London each have their own methods of predicting the future. But how much does God want us to know about the future?

Gen. 41: The Pharaoh has two dreams, and Joseph is brought out of prison to interpret them. He says that God is showing the Pharaoh by these dreams that Egypt will have seven years of good crops and then seven years of famine. Joseph also makes suggestions to the Pharaoh on how to prepare for the years of famine. The Pharaoh appoints Joseph himself as Minister of Agriculture. Joseph stores up food so well that when the famine begins there is enough food for everyone.

INTERPRETATION

We can probably interpret the stories about Joseph more easily than other stories in Genesis, for two reasons: first, because the writers state their interpretation plainly; second, because there is one great message behind all the stories about Joseph.

1. The great message is this: *God is at work in the things that happen* to Joseph. Nothing happened simply by chance. 'The Lord was with Joseph' (39.2). The Lord caused all that he did to prosper' (39.3). God was at work in the people surrounding the Pharaoh. See note below on Gen. 41.32, 'the thing is fixed by God'. Clearly God was with Joseph in prison. He not only gave Joseph comfort. He strengthened his character to endure the suffering, so that being stronger in character he was more able to serve God and other people.

2. God was using Joseph to save others. This is another important part of the message of these stories. Not only the Egyptians, but 'all the earth' had food to eat when the famine came (41.57). And later Joseph's own family came and were fed.

3. These are important stories for any Christian to read who is in difficulties or who is enduring suffering. He or she can say, 'God is with me in what is happening. I believe that God can use for good what I am suffering. God sees the place where He is leading me. He can bring good for other people out of the things that are now happening to me.'

NOTES

39.9. How then can I do this great wickedness, and sin against God? Joseph bravely refuses to do what Potiphar's wife asks him to do. He also explains to her what adultery is: it is not only a sin against people, but a sin against God Himself. All sin against people is sin against God, because the people are His children. And adultery is a wrong use of God's gift of sex. He did not give us sex for this. See Additional Note, Sin, p. 162.

40.8. Do not interpretations belong to God? In these words Joseph is speaking about dreams. (He says the same thing in 41.16, 'It is not in me'.) The words means that we shall understand our dreams best if we are in fellowship with God; for example, we can often learn truths about ourselves which we have not been willing to accept before and which God wants us to see.

But we need to avoid making mistakes in thinking about dreams, such as:

(a) laughing at them and refusing to see any meaning in them;

(b) thinking that only a magician can interpret them. This is what Pharaoh thought. He regarded Joseph as a magician;

(c) being distressed if we cannot interpret them. Often they are far too difficult to interpret.

41.32. The thing is fixed by God: (The AV has: 'the thing is established by God'.) Perhaps the writers thought that God had already 'fixed' or decided what events would take place. But God does not really work in that way. He has given us free will. Nor does it mean that when something happens God Himself has directly caused it. See notes on 6.7a; 19.25; 38.7. The truth is that God has established a great purpose for the world, and within that purpose He is actively at work in the hearts and minds of people. See Phil. 1.6.

Questions on Gen. 39—41

Words:

1. Read 39.9 and the Additional Note on Sin on p. 162 and give examples from everyday life to show the difference between 'sin' and (a) disaster (b) mistakes.

Content:

2. (a) Why was Joseph put in prison?
(b) Whose dreams did he interpret in prison?

3. 'God was using Joseph to save others' (p. 136). In what way and from what did Joseph save (a) The people of Egypt (b) the butler?

Bible:

4. Which events described in Gen. 39—41 are also described in (a) Ps. 105.17–22 (b) Acts 7.10, 11?

5. (i) What truth do we find in all the following passages?
(ii) Which person was the writer referring to in each case?
(a) Gen. 26.4 (b) Gen. 28.5 (c) Gen. 39.2 (d) Gen. 39.21 (e) 1 Sam. 3.19 (f) 1 Sam. 16.18.

Application:

6. 'The Lord was with Joseph' (Gen. 39.2). Are the following interpretations of these words true or false? Give reasons for your answer in each case.

(a) God was present with Joseph but absent from other people.

(b) Joseph was successful, so people said God must have shown him special favour.

(c) God was at work in the things that happened to Joseph, and He is at work in the things that happen to us.

7. We read on p. 136 that Joseph became 'stronger in character' through his sufferings.

(a) Why do some people become 'bitter' in suffering, but others become stronger in character?

(b) Give an example from everyday life of someone who becomes stronger.

(c) How could you help someone who was 'bitter'?

8. Israelites tried to obtain guidance about the future through magic (30.27), images (31.19) and dreams (40.12, 13).

(a) Should Christians seek guidance through any of those ways? Give your reasons.

(b) What are the best ways of seeking guidance about the future?

42, 43, 44, 45
Joseph and his Brothers

OUTLINE

Gen. 42: All Joseph's brothers except Benjamin come to Egypt to find food. They meet Joseph, but he pretends that he does not know them, and he cruelly accuses them of being spies. He tells them to go home and fetch Benjamin, who was his only full brother; then he puts Simeon in prison. At the same time he puts grain and money and food in their baggage. When the brothers find these they are afraid they will be accused of having stolen them.

Gen. 43: Jacob allows his sons to take Benjamin to Egypt with them, and they go back with him. They return the things that they had found in their baggage and Simeon is let out of prison. Then Joseph meets them and sees Benjamin; he provides them all with food.

"God sent me before you to preserve a remnant" (Gen. 45.7).

When miners from El Cobre, Chile, were buried and killed in an earthquake, there were very few survivors. But it is these survivors who will train the next generation of miners.

Gen. 44: Joseph again plays a trick on his brothers. When they are returning home, he puts money in their baggage and his own silver cup in Benjamin's. When this is found out, he pretends to arrest Benjamin. Judah asks to be arrested in place of Benjamin.

Gen. 45: Joseph at last tells his brothers who he is. He says that God sent him to Egypt, in order to 'preserve life'. He tells them to go home and to bring Jacob back with them. So they go home, and Jacob prepares to see Joseph.

INTERPRETATION

1. This passage contains its own interpretation in the words of Joseph (45.7, 8): 'God sent me before you to preserve for you a remnant on earth . . . So it was not you who sent me here, but God.'

We do not say that God made Joseph's brothers commit the sin of selling him to foreigners; we do not say that they were innocent; nor do we say that God made Joseph suffer in prison. But we do say that nothing was outside God's purpose. God knew what He wanted to do and He used the things that happened, the things which were caused by people's free will, in order that His purpose should be fulfilled. What did God want to do? To preserve His People, the Israelites, to make them into a strong nation, and, through them, to rescue the rest of humanity. This is what He has promised to do.

In this story God is preserving just one of His People, Joseph, as a way of preserving them all. The brothers had done wrong in selling Joseph, but through their sin he was taken into the land of plenty, into Egypt. See note on 45.7.

2. We have paid special attention above to what God was doing. But we should also notice the character of Joseph.

Joseph forgave his brothers for what they had done to him. We do right to rejoice at this, and to rejoice every time one human being forgives another. But there is a forgiving which is even harder than Joseph's. He forgave people after he had become successful in spite of their sin. Forgiving someone who has caused our downfall is even more difficult. Yet through Christ even this is possible for us.

NOTES

42.18. I fear God: To 'fear' sometimes means to 'be terrified of' or 'not to trust'. But Joseph was not terrified of God, nor did he distrust Him. 'Fear' also means 'respect and reverence and desire to obey'. This is what Joseph meant by these words. Fear or respect of the Lord is the 'beginning of wisdom' (Psalm 111.10; Prov. 9.10).

42.22. Now there comes a reckoning for his blood: This is one of many verses in which the brothers show that they realize they are guilty. See also 44.16.

Reuben said this because he thought that Joseph was dead. But his words contain a truth which we find in the New Testament (see Gal. 6.7). We know that when we have sinned we can be forgiven through Jesus. But we also know that the sinful deed can bring its own punishment upon the sinner. Christians who obtain leadership in a congregation chiefly in order to obtain power over others may seem successful at first; but after a time they are likely to find members fall away and they are left with no one to rule over. Then there has come 'a reckoning'.

44.5. By this . . . he divines: One of the ways in which people believed they could tell the future was by means of a cup. It was filled with water and then precious stones were dropped into it. The future was told by noticing what shadows could be seen on the side of the cup. This still continues among 'diviners' and oracles and magicians in many parts of the world. This sort of 'divining' was once practised by the Israelites and later was forbidden among them (Deut. 18.10). It was forbidden because people who trust God have no need of such ways. Generally speaking, God does not seem to intend us to know about the future; He says that He will take care of us, and calls upon us to trust Him.

The Egyptians clearly regarded Joseph as a 'diviner', but we do not know if he really used such methods.

45.5a. Do not be . . . angry with yourselves: We know that we should forgive other people, although it is not easy. But we often forget that we must learn how to forgive ourselves. If we are sincerely sorry for a sin, and confess it to God, we believe that He forgives us. So it is wrong to try to be more severe than God and to refuse to forgive ourselves. See 1 John 3.19–21.

45.5b. God sent me before you to preserve life: The events had not taken place by chance. God was continually at work in the lives of His servants. The writers of Genesis have shown this many times.

45.7. God sent me . . . to preserve a remnant: The teaching behind this verse is behind all the stories about Joseph, namely, that God used the things that happened, and used them so that good resulted. Christians should not be surprised to read that God used human sin. Crucifying Jesus was a very great sin, but God used it as the way by which His people are made new. But if God used the things that happened (which at the time caused suffering), He uses the things that are happening now. He has not changed. See Additional Note, Remnant, p. 160.

Questions on Gen. 42—45

Words:

1. Read the Additional Note on Remnant on p. 160.

(a) Who was the 'remnant' according to 45.7?

(b) Why did God rescue that remnant?

(c) Who was the remnant in Jer. 6.9 and Micah 2.12?

(d) Who are now the remnant according to Rom. 11.1–12?

Content:

2. Why did Jacob send his sons to Egypt?

3. (a) What special relationship did Joseph have with Benjamin?

(b) How did he show this relationship?

4. What does 'fear' mean in 42.18?

Bible:

5. In what way is the situation described in Gen. 42.8 like the situation described in Luke 24.16?

6. In what way are the following two statements alike: Gen. 45.5a and 1 John 3.20?

Application:

7. Joseph forgave his brothers.

(a) In your experience when is forgiving most difficult?

(b) What can help us to forgive others?

(c) How far is it possible for a whole group of people to forgive, e.g. a nation or a class of students?

(d) When we fail to forgive others, who is most harmed, others or ourselves? Explain.

8. The Egyptians thought that Joseph foretold the future by means of a cup (44.5).

(a) What other ways, traditional or modern, do people use to foretell the future?

(b) Which ways should Christians avoid? Give reasons.

9. 'When we have sinned we can be forgiven through Jesus. But . . . the sinful deed can bring its own punishment' (p. 141). A schoolboy stole some books from the wife of his headmaster and then lost them. When it was discovered, the headmaster told the boy that he fully forgave him but that he would have to pay for the books. The boy said, 'If you make me pay, then you have not forgiven me.'

(a) What is your opinion?

(b) What difference would it have made if the headmaster had not forgiven the boy?

10. 'God used things that happened (which at the time caused suffering), He uses the things that are happening now. He has not changed' (p. 141). What things are happening now which cause suffering but which God can use? How can we be part of God's work?

46, 47, 48
Jacob comes to Egypt

OUTLINE

This passage is a collection of stories, from different writers, which the editors have put together.

46.1–7: Jacob leaves Hebron to go to Egypt. On the journey he has a vision, in which God says to him, 'I will go down with you to Egypt.'

46.8–27: A list of Jacob's descendants.

46.28—47.12: There is a famine in Canaan. So Jacob travels to Egypt, and meets Joseph, whom he has not seen for over twenty years. Then Jacob and five of his sons meet the Pharaoh, and the Pharaoh allows them to settle in Goshen on the East of the Nile Delta.

47.13–27: Joseph continues his work as Minister of Agriculture. When the famine becomes very severe, the people sell their land to the Pharaoh and become his slaves.

47.28–31: Jacob is dying, and Joseph promises to bury him in Canaan.

Gen. 48: Joseph brings his sons, Manasseh and Ephraim, to be blessed by Jacob. Jacob first adopts them as his own sons, then blesses them, giving the chief blessing to the younger son, Ephraim. Finally, he blesses Joseph.

INTERPRETATION

The important part of this passage is the last part. In this part Jacob passes on the blessing which he had received from Isaac, and gives it to a son of Joseph's (48.14). Then he says to Joseph, 'God . . . will bring you again to the land of your fathers' (48.21). The editors have thus given us once again the following truth: *God's purpose is being carried out. His promise is being kept.* As one member of the Chosen People dies, another takes his place. And God's promise to give them a land of their own will be kept too. God is working His purpose out.

Note: Jacob is also called 'Israel', e.g. in 46.1, 2, 8, 29.

NOTES

46.6. They . . . came into Egypt: Jacob and his family went to Egypt to get food. The editors recorded the story to point to a greater truth than this. Being Jews themselves, they did not think of Egypt chiefly as a country; they thought of it as the place where God showed His power to rescue His People. When the Israelites became slaves there, God brought them out at the Exodus, at the time of the Passover. No Jew who believes in God has ever forgotten that. All through the Bible the writers were thinking of that when they referred to 'Egypt'. The Passover is still the great Jewish festival. See Mark 14.1.

46.8. These are the names of the descendants: The writer says that these are the people who entered Egypt with Jacob. But this is really a list of Jacob's descendants. Gen. 46.19 shows this, for it contains the name of Joseph who was already in Egypt. And there are others in the list who did not go with Jacob at that time.

Who did go to Egypt with Jacob? The list says 'seventy people' (46.27), but it is likely that a much bigger number went.

Some readers are troubled, because there are contradictions in these chapters. According to 46.21 Benjamin had ten sons at that time, but according to 44.33 he was still a young boy. The reason for this is probably that 46.21 is by the Priestly Writer, and 44.33 comes from another writer.

47.21. He made slaves of them: When the famine was very bad indeed, the people had no more money and no more cattle. They were forced to sell themselves as well as their land to the Pharaoh in order to get food. So they became his slaves, and he owned all the land in Egypt except what the priests owned.

The editors of this chapter were probably living, or had been living in exile in Babylon, under Nebuchadnezzar, deprived of their freedom. As they edited this chapter and interpreted it, they surely had in mind the many other oppressed peoples who were waiting for liberation (as indeed are many peoples today). They, like those others, lived under a wealthy ruler who misused his power and made profit out of the people's poverty. See 47.14: 'brought the money into Pharaoh's house'.

48.14. Crossing his hands: Joseph expected that Jacob would put his right hand on the elder son, Manasseh, because the chief blessing was given with the right hand. So he put Manasseh in front of Jacob's right hand. But Jacob crossed his hands and gave the chief blessing to the younger son Ephraim.

Perhaps this story was written down because it explains why the tribe of Ephraim became more important than the tribe of Manasseh. Certainly Ephraim did become the stronger tribe.

But there is a greater truth behind the story; again and again God does not choose the person whom people expect to be chosen. David, not any of his seven older brothers, was chosen (1 Sam. 16.7–12). God had chosen what the world considers weakness (1 Cor. 1.27). People are continually surprised by God. As St Paul said, the 'man' who was despised and crucified has become exalted and is 'Lord' (Phil. 2.9–11). So the editors of Gen. 48 are saying that God's choices are surprising.

48.19. He also shall become a people: The word 'people' here means much more than a number of men and women. It stands for the 'people whom God has chosen for a special purpose'. See Additional Note, People of God, p. 159.

Questions on Gen. 46—48

Words:

1. Read Gen. 48.19 and the Additional Note on 'People' (p. 159).

   (a) Who, according to Acts 13.16, 17, said that God chose Abraham's descendants to be a special *People*?

   (b) What was the agreement called by which the Israelites were God's *'People'*?

   (c) For what purpose did God make them His *People*?

   (d) Who are 'God's *People*' today according to 1 Pet. 2.9 and 10?

Content:

2. Why did Jacob go to Egypt?

3. Why was he glad to see Joseph?

4. (a) What was Joseph's great work in Egypt?

   (b) How far did his previous life prepare him for that work?

Bible:

5. What great event concerning Egypt did the writers of the following passages have in mind? Exod. 13.14; Ps. 105.37, 38; Heb. 8.9a.

6. 'Again and again God does not choose the person whom people expect to be chosen . . . God's choices are surprising' (p. 145). Read the following passages and say if you would call God's choice 'surprising': (a) Gen. 48.14 (b) 1 Sam. 16.7–12 (c) Mark 10.14 (d) Luke 15.20–30 (e) Phil. 2.8, 9.

Application:
7. 'He made slaves of them' (47.21).

(a) In which parts of the world are there still slaves?

(b) Describe any people of which you know who are treated by employers as if they owned them.

(c) What laws exist to make employers treat their workers fairly?

(d) Should the Church ask for new laws to overcome injustice where injustice exists?

Special Note E:
The Stories about Joseph

Most of the stories we have been reading in Gen. 37—48 are about Joseph. Why have people found these stories so important that they handed them down? Here are some of the reasons:

1. Because they are very good stories. They are written in such a way that people of all ages and in all countries enjoy telling them and hearing them.
2. Because they tell us something about the history of Israelite tribes of that time. When the writers tell us about Joseph, they are also telling us about the life of the whole tribe of Joseph. When other brothers join Joseph we are reading how other tribes joined the tribe of Joseph in Egypt, and thus how Abraham's descendants became a great nation in Egypt.
3. Because they give us a picture of a very good person. He was good in so many ways that we may make the mistake of reading these stories in order to imitate him. But this would be a mistake because they contain a much greater lesson.
4. Because they show that God uses the sufferings of His People as a way of rescuing others. This is the chief reason why these stories are important. In this way they prepare us for many of the great events of which we read in the rest of the Bible. For example, when the Israelites were taken into exile in Babylon, God used their sufferings while they were there, and some of them discovered that they could become a 'light to the nations' (Isa. 49.6). When we come to the New Testament and read of the sufferings and death of Jesus, we see that God used His sufferings and death as the way by which we may all be rescued from the results of our sin.

Questions on Special Note E

1. A child who is unwell has asked you to tell a story. Which story from the life of Joseph would you choose? Why would you choose that one?

2. 'The mistake of reading these stories in order to imitate him' (p. 147). Why is it a mistake to use stories about Joseph in that way?

3. 'God uses the sufferings of His People' (p. 147). (i) What did

'God uses the sufferings of His people as a way of rescuing others' (p. 147).

Janani Luwum, Archbishop of Uganda, boldly protested to President Idi Amin that his rule was causing sufferings and death throughout the country. Because of this protest he was murdered, but, as a result of his martyrdom, changes began to take place in Uganda.

each of the following suffer, and (ii) In what way did God use their suffering? (a) Joseph (b) The Israelites in Babylon (c) Jesus (d) Paul, according to Phil. 1.12–14.

4. Mention two events in Joseph's life which seem to you to be like events in Jesus' life.

49, 50
The Last Days of Jacob and Joseph

OUTLINE

There are three parts to this passage:

49.1–28: We read here that Jacob pronounced certain sayings before he died. At first they seem to be about his twelve sons, but we learn from 49.28 that they are about the twelve tribes.

49.29—50.14: The story of Jacob's death. After his death his body is embalmed and taken to Machpelah, near Hebron in Canaan, where Abraham and Isaac had also been buried. Then Joseph returns to Egypt.

50.15–end: After Jacob's death, his sons are afraid that Joseph will punish them for the wrong they did to him. But he assures them that he has forgiven them. Although their deed was evil, God has used it for good (50.20). Then he tells them that God will one day lead His People back to their own country (50.24). Then Joseph dies.

INTERPRETATION

Behind the story of the deaths of Jacob and Joseph we must again notice two great truths which we noticed throughout the stories about Joseph. Indeed the whole Bible shows them to be true.

1. *God is in charge.* His purpose is not defeated by evil deeds. Indeed He can use them in order to produce good. See 50.20, 21. We need not be anxious.

2. *God keeps His promises.* We can trust Him. He will keep His promise to bring His People into the land which He has prepared for them. 'God will visit you, and bring you up out of this land to the land which He swore to Abraham, to Isaac, and to Jacob' (50.24).

149

NOTES

49.1. Jacob called his sons and said: Gen. 49 consists of the 'sayings of Jacob'. People have interpreted the chapter in different ways:

1. As a story of Jacob *foretelling* the future: we could pick out 49.1, 'I may tell you what shall befall'.

2. As Jacob's *blessing* of his sons: we could pick out the words from 49.28: 'He blessed them'. But 49.3–7 are not blessings, and 49.7 is a curse.

3. As a *description* of what happened to the twelve tribes of the Israelites, which was written down after Jacob's death. Those who read Gen. 49 in Hebrew say that it seems much more like a carefully written poem or psalm than the words of a man just before his death. They also point out that according to 49.28 it is about the twelve tribes, not about the sons.

If we accept this third interpetation, we may ask why the editors included it in the Book of Genesis. One answer is that it was their way of saying, 'What has happened to the twelve tribes has not happened simply by chance.' Today we might express the same thing by writing: 'God was not ignorant of what was happening to the twelve tribes. He was able to use both their obedience and their disobedience to fulfil his purposes for all people.'

49.10b. Until he comes to whom it belongs; and to him shall be the obedience of the peoples: The first half of this verse clearly says that the tribe of Judah will be the leader among the tribes. But the meaning of 49.10b is not clear. 'Until he comes' may mean 'until a great leader comes from the tribe of Judah'. Or perhaps the writers were looking forward to the time when God would send His Messiah. One of the Dead Sea Scrolls (manuscripts from a Jewish sect which existed in the time of Jesus' ministry) interprets the words in this way.

50.2. The physicians embalmed Israel; 50.26. Joseph died . . . and they embalmed him: We read in 50.3 that embalming took forty days, and we know that an embalmed body or 'mummy' lasts for thousands of years without becoming decayed. Christians should pay respect to the body of someone who has died. But when they do so they know that they cannot in this way bring greater peace to him. This peace is something that God alone can give. A Christian funeral is a time of committing the person who has died into God's hands. The body returns to nature, of which it is a part.

50.20. You meant evil against me, but God meant it for good . . . that many people should be kept alive: Many Jews have interpreted this verse as a prediction that the Jews would be delivered from exile in Babylon. Christians see the words being fulfilled in the death and resurrection of Jesus. People treated Jesus in evil ways, but the result of His life and death was that 'many' have been and are being given new life.

50.24. God will visit you, and bring you up out of this land: See Additional Note, Visit, p. 163.

The last thing that Joseph did was to affirm his faith in the power and love of God. 'God will keep His promises,' he was saying, 'and fulfil His plans.' Like Joseph we do not know what the future holds; but we do know Who holds the future.

Questions on Gen. 49 and 50

Content:

1. What two truths about God can we discover in Genesis 49 and 50?

2. What were Joseph's brothers afraid of?

3. For what reason did the Egyptians embalm dead bodies?

Bible:

4. What interpretation of Gen. 50.24, 25 does the writer of Heb. 11.22 give?

5. Read the Additional Note on Visit on p. 163 and the following passages, and say in each case,

(i) whom God visited;

(ii) whether God's visit resulted in 'salvation' or in 'punishment'.

(a) Gen. 50.24 (b) Exod. 32.31–4 (c) 1 Sam 2.21 (d) Isa. 26.13, 14 (e) Acts 15.14–18

6. In what way is the teaching in each of the following passages the same or nearly the same?

Gen. 3.5b   Gen. 50.19b   Isa. 40.18–20   Isa. 45.9   Acts 12.21, 22

Application:

7. 'Christians should pay respect to the body of someone who has died' (p. 150). Do you agree? Give reasons for your answer.

8. They embalmed the body of Jacob and wept for him for seventy days.

(a) Describe the actions of any non-Christians whom you know when one of them dies.

(b) What can you learn about their beliefs by studying what they do?

(c) What would a non-Christian think about Christian beliefs after studying the behaviour of people at a Christian funeral? (If possible, refer to an actual funeral you have attended.)

ADDITIONAL NOTES
ON IMPORTANT WORDS

We give below notes on twenty words used in the Book of Genesis. The words are given in alphabetical order.

Angel
Chief references: Gen. 3.24; 18.1–15; 19.1–23; 24.7; 28.12; 32.1, 2; 32.22–32.
Notes: pp. 38, 96, 106, 122.
The word 'angel' does not mean the same thing each time it is used.

1. Sometimes an angel is a messenger bringing words from God. By speaking of an angel in these passages, the writers were telling us that God sends us guidance, as in 16.7–13; 18; 19; 22.11; 24.7, 40; and 31.11.
Sometimes an angel brings protection. In such passages the writers were describing the protection which God gives. See 21.17 and 48.16.
2. So when we read about angels, we are reading about God Himself. And we are reading something important about God, namely that He is interested in our affairs and concerns Himself with them. This is especially clear in 19.15; 21.17; 32.1, 2; 32.28.
3. Why did the writers use the word 'angel'? Why did they not use the name of God? They used the word 'angel' because they felt that God was too great, too high, sometimes too dangerous. When communication took place, it had to be through a being who was less than God Himself. See 16.11–13.
4. By writing about angels, the writers are telling truths about God which could not have been expressed in any other way. These truths are: He guides us; He protects us; although He is 'high and lifted up', He has communication with us.
5. In some passages it is not clear whether the writers are telling us about angels or about human beings. One reason for this is that the Hebrew word *malak* means a messenger, either an angel or a human being. But even when the writers are clearly referring to angels they do not always use the word *malak*.

Anger (of God)
Chief references: 18.30; 18.32.
Notes: pp. 96, 97.
When writers say that God was 'angry', they are not saying that God was hot-tempered or that God could not control His anger. They are saying:

1. God is not neutral towards sin. He is against it (see Mark 11.15–18). He could not save us if He were not against it. This attitude is called His 'anger'. See Additional Note on Judgement, p. 156.

2. But God is merciful as well as angry. He allows people to suffer as a result of their sin, but at the same time provides a way by which they can be restored to fellowship with Him. See Habakkuk 3.2.

Blessing (of God)
Chief references: 1.22; 1.28; 9.1; 12.2, 3; 22.17; 26.3; 27.7; 27.29; 28.13–15; 32.26–9; 39.5.
Notes: pp. 16, 63, 84, 85, 112–113.

1. God's 'blessing' is twofold:
(a) His goodwill: i.e. He desires the best things for us, goodness and happiness, because of His love and goodwill.
(b) His power: i.e. He has the power actually to give such things.
2. We can see a difference between the blessings God gives to everyone and the special blessings He gives to His Chosen People:
(a) In 1.22 and 9.1, we see His blessings given for everyone.
(b) In the story of Abraham (12.1–3) and in the story about Isaac giving God's blessing to Jacob, we see His special blessings, i.e. God had a special purpose for His Chosen People and gave them special protection.

We also see that a human being can speak a blessing on behalf of God, e.g. in 27.1–29; 48.14.

Blood
Chief references: 4.10, 11; 9.4–6.
Note: p. 65.
When a living creature loses a lot of blood, its life comes to an end. So it has often been said that 'the life is the blood' (see Gen. 9.4; Lev. 17.11). This explains two customs of the Israelites:

1. The custom of not eating meat which still had blood in it.
2. The custom of sacrificing an animal and sprinkling its blood on two people who were making an agreement.

Among many peoples today agreements are still made by means of blood. There are, for example, two small tribes who wish to live in close friendship with each other. In order that this unity shall continue, every year boys from one of the tribes mix some of their blood with the blood of boys from the other tribe. In the same way the Israelites believed that two people making an agreement according to this custom were united, because both were touched with the same life. In the Letter to the Hebrews the writer used this custom to explain the result of Jesus' death. He said that when Jesus 'shed His blood', God and human

154

beings came to share the same life, and fellowship became possible between them (Heb. 9.12–28).

Circumcision

Chief references: 17.9–14; 17.22–7; 21.4; 34.13–24.
Notes: pp. 18, 93, 94, 125, 127.

1. People have practised circumcision for thousands of years, especially in desert regions such as the country in which Abraham made his journeys. At first they probably practised it in order to avoid discomfort and disease. But later it became a common preparation for marriage, as it is among many peoples today.

2. We might think from reading Gen. 17 that circumcision only began among Israelites in the time of Abraham, but they had probably practised it long before that time. (There is no reference to female circumcision in the Bible.)

3. According to Gen. 17 it marked the Covenant between God and Abraham and His People the Israelites. It continued to have this meaning, and when the Israelites were taken into exile into Babylon 900 or 1,000 years later, it was the chief sign that they were different from most other tribes.

4. It was a good practice because it helped to remind the Israelites to avoid the heathen customs of other nations. But they often became too proud of their circumcision, as if it made them superior to other people. So the prophets had to remind them that it was a sign that they were dedicated to God and tied to Him by the Covenant.

5. Christians have no rule about it.

(a) St Paul, writing to Christian Jews, could still use a circumcised man as a picture of one who is in his heart dedicated to God (Rom. 2.29).

(b) But in Rom. 4.9, 10 St Paul shows that Abraham was accepted by God because he had faith, and *before* he was circumcised. From this he says that God accepts anyone who has faith, and that circumcision itself is no longer necessary.

Covenant

Chief references: 6.18; 9.8–17; 15.18; 17.1–21.
Notes: pp. 2, 60, 63, 65, 66, 90–94.

1. Writers in the Bible use this word to describe an agreement which binds God and human beings together; it shows that God has not abandoned us, and will never do so.

2. In 9.8–17 we read of the covenant which God has with everyone. This covenant, made with Noah, still exists between God and all peoples. (See Interpretation and Notes on 8.21—9.17).

3. The covenant of which we read in Genesis 15 and 17 is between

God and a chosen section of humanity, i.e. Abraham and his descendants. We also read of other covenants which God made with them later (e.g. in Exodus 19).

4. In these covenants we notice three things:

(a) God took the first step in making them. He did it simply because He cares for those whom He has created.

(b) They were not agreements between equals, such as an agreement between one man who is selling a cow and one who is buying it. They were more like the agreement between dying people and their family; they say who shall have their possessions: they and the family do not meet as equals.

(c) In a covenant each person must take some part. The part taken by Noah and Abraham was to accept and obey what God said. When someone is baptized God makes His promises and the candidates mark their willingness to accept and obey.

5. The Israelites often forgot the promises they had made to God; they forgot that they had promised to obey Him by the uprightness of their lives. So Jeremiah said that a 'New Covenant' would be made between God and His People (Jer. 31.31–4).

6. Then Jesus came, and by His death made this 'New Covenant' between God and His people which takes the place of the old one (Mark 14.24). This is why the two parts of the Bible are called the Old Covenant and the New Covenant ('testament' is another word for 'covenant').

So Christians live by the covenant made through Jesus. Each person can say, 'I belong to God: He belongs to me.'

Curse

Chief references: 3.14–17; 4.11; 9.25; 12.3; 27.12, 13, 29.

Notes: pp. 36, 37, 44, 45, 68–70, 111–113.

When writers say that God 'cursed' someone, they are not saying that God had ceased to love that person. Nor are they saying that anyone is cursed by God before birth.

They are saying that that person has been offered God's blessing, but has refused it. See Additional Note on Blessing, p. 154. The one who has sinned will suffer the results of sin. See Additional Note on Judgement. See also 5.29.

Jesus took on Himself the result of human sinfulness. This is why St Paul said that Jesus had become 'a curse' for us (Gal. 3.13).

Judgement

Chief references: 15.14; 18.25; 31.53.

Notes: pp. 35, 53, 54.

1. God judges us because He loves us and wants justice to be done. The writers of the Bible are glad that God is a judge, because He is a just one.

2. He judges us throughout our lives; every day is a judgement day. But at the end of the history of human beings, there will be the last and great day of judgement.

3. Sinful people suffer and are punished because God judges. In Genesis the word 'punish' is not used, but these words are used: 'curse' (3.14), 'drive out' (3.24), 'destroy' (6.13), 'be angry' (18.30). These words show that the result of sin is disaster. (It may fall on the person who sins, or it may fall on others, because we all belong to each other.)

4. We can say, therefore, that people punish themselves. To say this is not to deny that God is judge. God made the world in such a way that this happens, and He goes on letting it happen.

5. Judgement is not the end of God's relationship with sinners. As God punishes sinners He works to bring them back into fellowship with Him. Indeed, He punishes those sinners *in order* to restore fellowship between them. God is merciful as well as just.

Life
Chief references: 1.30; 2.7; 3.20–4; 9.3–5.
Notes: pp. 24, 37, 65, 92.
The English word 'life' has been used to translate such Hebrew words as *nephesh* and *chaiyim*.

1. All living creatures have life because God has given His own life to them.

2. This is true of the kind of life that human beings and animals share (1.24; 2.7). This is the life that comes to an end when they die.

3. Writers of the Bible did not think of a person's life as being divided into different parts as we often do today, e.g. we may speak of 'body, mind and spirit'. See Additional Note on Man, para. 2. For this reason the best English translation of the Hebrew word *nephesh* is often 'self' or 'person'. (*Nephesh* has often been translated 'soul', but this is misleading. Today we use the word 'soul' to refer to the way that someone responds to God.)

4. There is another sort of life which is the gift of God to us, namely the full life of being in fellowship with God (Deut. 30.19). In St John's Gospel we see that this 'full' life is what Jesus came to give (John 10.10). It is a life which we can have now, and which no one can take away because it is 'eternal' (John 5.24).

Man, meaning Humanity
Chief references: 1.26, 27; 2.7; 3.8–24; 5.1, 2; 6.4–7; 11.1–5.
Notes: pp. 1, 3, 12, 13, 18, 21, 23, 24, 30–34, 42, 53, 63–71, 78, 80.

1. Human beings belong to each other: the ways in which they are the same as each other are more important than the ways in which they are different. There is more teaching in the Bible, especially in Genesis 1—11, about human beings than about separate people. The word 'Adam' refers to all of us.

2. When human beings are referred to, they are regarded as living beings who show that they are alive in many ways. The words 'flesh', 'spirit', 'body', 'heart', 'mind', 'soul' may show what these different ways are. But each of these words can refer to the whole person or personality. Not even the writers of Deut. 10.12, who use a phrase like 'heart and . . . soul', thought of a person as divided up into parts, as we often do today. And God Himself treats each of us as a whole person.

3. Human beings are different from other creatures of God. They are made 'in God's image' (see 1.26; 5.1, 3; 9.6). They can have fellowship with God. They are responsible for other creatures (1.28). This is how God intends people to be, and is described in Gen. 1 and 2.

4. But people are also sinful. They forget that they are God's creatures. They act as if they, and not God, were in authority. See notes on 2.17; 3.5; 11.4a and 4b.

5. So human beings are *both* in God's image *and* at the same time weak and sinful. They have some of their 'original goodness', but they also have their 'original sin'. They are spoilt, but not completely spoilt.

6. Thus, we human beings are capable of being saved from sin. This is the first piece of good news about us. The other good news is that God has made it possible for this saving to take place. Jesus Christ was born as the 'second Adam', i.e. He was what human beings were created to be. Through Him all of us can be created again (2 Cor. 5.19).

Name
Chief references: 2.19, 20; 4.26; 12.2, 8; 13.4; 17.5; 32.27–9; 35.10.
Notes: pp. 28, 29, 88–90.
A name is sometimes just a convenient way of showing that one person is not the same as another person: 'This is "Jacob", that is "Esau".'

But when writers in the Bible refer to someone's name they are often referring to their character and to their powers.

1. God's 'Name' stands for the character of God as people know it from the actions of God which they have seen. In 12.8; 13.4; 21.33, Abraham 'called on the Name of the Lord', i.e. he worshipped God, knowing God's character from the protection which He had given to him.

2. To give names to people often means to know them and understand them, and therefore to have power over them. So when Adam gave names to the animals he had control over them (Gen. 2.20).

3. When people's position or character was changed, often their

'name' was changed, e.g. Abraham's (17.5), Jacob's (32.28). So those who are baptized as Christians are given a new name to show their new position and status in the world.

People of God
Chief references: 12.2; 46.3; 48.19.
Notes: pp. 84, 145.

1. In this note we shall study the *fact* that there was a people specially chosen by God, rather than the Hebrew words which are translated 'people'. (The Hebrew word *am* is usually translated 'people', and usually refers to the Chosen People; the Hebrew word *goi* is translated 'nation', and usually refers to the nations other than Israelites. But sometimes, as in 12.2, *goi* refers to the Chosen People.)
2. In the Old Testament the 'People' are described in this way:
(a) They are Abraham and his descendants.
(b) They were chosen by God. Passages like 12.2; 17.1–14; 18.18 show this, although the words 'choose', 'elect', 'call' are not used.
(c) They became His People through the Covenant. In this Covenant, God made promises to them to protect them and to give them a place in which to live. Their part in the Covenant was to obey and serve Him.
(d) They were chosen in order that, through them, God might rescue all people from the results of sin (12.3b).
3. When God made a New Covenant through Jesus Christ, those with whom He made it were the new People of God (1 Peter 2.9, 10).
4. Christians have the privilege of being the new People, but they also have their responsibilities. They have been chosen for special work in the world, to be 'servants' of all, to be 'salt' in the world. They are not better than other people; they serve a better Master.

Remember
Chief references: 8.1; 9.15, 16; 19.29; 30.22.
Note: p. 61, 62.
When we are told that God 'remembered Noah' (8.1), it does not mean that a thought about Noah came into God's mind. Nor does it mean that God had forgotten about him until this time. It means that God showed His mercy to Noah in a special way. Compare this with the use of the word 'remember' in the following sentences: 'My uncle remembered me in his will', i.e. he left me money; 'She remembered my birthday', i.e. she gave me a present.
The word often means this in the Bible, especially in the phrase: 'God remembered His Covenant' (see 9.15, 16). This means, 'Because of the promises God had made in the Covenant, He took action and

rescued His people.' It has the same meaning in the words of Mary in Luke 1.54, and in the words of Zechariah in Luke 1.72.

Remnant
Reference: 45.7.
Notes: pp. 54, 139, 140, 142.

1. In the Bible writers sometimes use this word to describe some soldiers who happened to escape when others were killed.

2. But usually it refers to those members of the human race who, according to the plan of God, were saved from destruction. Noah and his wife were that sort of 'remnant'. See Interpretation and Notes on 6.5–10.

3. Three more facts should be noticed:

(a) The word is especially used for the Chosen People, or rather for those of them who were rescued in order that they might do God's work. See Isa. 1.9 and Ezra 9.8.

(b) They were rescued in order that they should rescue others (45.7).

(c) Finally, at the time of Jesus Christ, the 'remnant' is one Person, Jesus Himself. He is rescued from death and raised to life in order that He may rescue others from sin.

Sacrifice
Chief references: 4.3–5; 8.20; 14.18; 15.9; 22.1–13; 31.54; 35.14; 46.1.
Notes: pp. 42–45, 89, 92–93, 101–104.

1. The Israelites regarded sacrifice chiefly as a way which God had given them by which they could approach Him. They also used it in making agreements between two people.

Sometimes an animal was killed; sometimes food, wine, oil or cereal was offered. Sometimes the sacrifice was made privately, sometimes in public by a priest.

2. The Israelites approached God by sacrifice for various reasons:

(a) To give something to God, e.g. in thanksgiving. See 4.3 (Cain's harvest offering), and 22.1–13 (Abraham's attempt to make a burnt-offering of his son and his sacrifice of a ram).

(b) To keep up their friendship with God. See 8.20 (Noah's sacrifice), and 31.54 (Jacob and Laban made an agreement and completed it by sacrificing to God).

(c) To ask for help before a difficult piece of work. See 46.1.

(d) To ask for forgiveness (a 'sin-offering').

(e) To complete a covenant which was being made between God and humans.

3. Jesus made the perfect offering to God when He came and died on the cross. By His death a 'New Covenant' was made between God and

human beings, and sacrifices were no longer needed. See Hebrews 9 and 10, especially 9.26 and 10.10.

Christians today approach God for some of the same reasons for which sacrifices were made in the old days, e.g. to thank Him, to ask for forgiveness, etc. But we approach Him 'through Jesus Christ our Lord'.

Save

Reference: 45.7.

Notes: pp. 44, 48, 54, 57–61, 95.

1. There are two or three Hebrew words which are translated in the RSV by such words as 'save' and 'deliver' and 'redeem' and 'heal'. These words show that God is active on behalf of us. He not only loves; He also has power to help.

2. We see this truth in the Bible through stories as well as through words. In Genesis such stories are:

(a) God provides clothes for Adam and Eve (3.21).

(b) He puts a mark on Cain (4.15).

(c) He shows Noah how to make an ark (6.14).

(d) He rescues Joseph from the pit and from the prison (45.7).

The whole Bible is the story of God's saving or rescuing humanity. But the story which the Jews have regarded as the most important is God's saving of their ancestors from Egypt (Exod. 12).

3. In the Old and New Testaments we learn three things about God's saving:

(a) God alone can save, but He uses people through whom to do His work of saving. e.g. He used Moses in order to save the Israelites from Egypt.

(b) God saves us from the greatest of all evils, namely from living like strangers in the presence of God. He does not promise to save us from all pain and evil in this world. But we read in the Bible of some people who did expect God to save those who were righteous from loneliness and starvation, e.g. in Ps. 37.25.

(c) He saves people so that they may save other people. See Note on 12.3.

4. What God did, He still does. Through Him it is possible for us here and now to be saved. See 2 Tim. 1.9.

5. And yet our 'salvation' cannot be completed until the Last Judgement. See 2 Tim. 4.18.

See also Additional Notes on Blessing, Remember, Steadfast love, Visit.

Say (also Speak, Word, etc.)

Chief references: 1.3; 3.9; 3.14; 4.6a; 15.1–5; 22.1.

Notes: pp. 8, 36, 43, 94, 103, 104.

'Say' and 'speak' (as well as such other words as 'tell' and 'word') have a double meaning.

1. The first meaning is that 'speaking' gives information or a message or a greeting to the hearer. While showing what sort of person the speaker is, it shows what the will of that person is.

When we read that 'God spoke' we are not being told that God has lips like ours, or that He made sounds as we do. The writers are telling us that God is willing to make Himself known, and His will known, to us men and women. He does not wait for us to discover Him.

2. The second meaning is that 'speaking', according to writers of the Bible, leads to action. It has power, and the thing that the speaker wants to be done is done. 'God said, "Let there be light", And there was light' (1.3). 'He spoke, and it came to be' (Psalm 33.9).

3. As God speaks, He waits for our reply. Our reply is our life.

From the above it is clear why St John describes Jesus as 'the Word' which had become flesh (John 1.14). First of all, Jesus had brought people a message about God, and about the relationship which is possible between God and ourselves. Secondly, He actually *did* the work of rescuing: the word led to action.

Sin

Chief references: 2.17; 3.1–24; 4.1–9; 6.5–12; 13.13; 18.20; 31.36; 39.9; 50.17.

Notes: pp. 2, 25, 26, 30–39, 42, 45, 53–57, 63, 78, 121, 136, 137.

1. Those who use the word 'sin' are sometimes thinking of it as a bad condition or a sort of disease, and they speak of 'sinfulness'. Sometimes they are thinking of it as an action, and they speak of it as 'a sin'.

(a) It is a sort of disease which affects everything we do, just as some sicknesses of the body affect every action of the ill person. This is the condition of being divided within ourselves: we partly acknowledge God's authority and partly reject it.

Thus sin does not only lead to someone else being harmed; sinners themselves are harmed.

(b) Sin is also an action. A sinful action breaks the agreement or 'covenant' between God and human beings. It also breaks the understanding between one person and another person (see 39.9). So sin is much more serious than breaking a rule or a human law. (A 'crime' is breaking the law of the country, and so is not the same as sin).

2. Sin is in all human beings. The first humans were sinful and so are we. This is what the writers are saying in Gen. 3. They are not saying

that we sin because Adam sinned, and that therefore we can blame Adam rather than ourselves. (But it is true, of course, that our behaviour is strongly influenced by those who have lived before us.)

As to the question, 'Where does sin come from?' there is no one direct answer in the Bible.

3. Sin results in suffering. Sometimes it brings suffering to the sinners themselves, sometimes to others. Some results of sin are described in Gen. 3, e.g. the suffering of guilt (3.8), the suffering of separation 3.24). See Additional Note on Judgement. But we are *not* told that all suffering is the result of sin.

4. But God is not defeated by sin. God has not cut Himself off from us, even though readers of 3.24 ('He drove out the man') might think that that is what God has done. We know from the teaching of Jesus that God is continually working to rescue us from our sin and from the results of it. This is why He created His Chosen People. Jesus belonged to that people, and because of His obedience and His dying we need never be overwhelmed by sin.

Steadfast love
Chief references: 24.12–14; 24.27; 32.10; 39.21.
Notes: pp. 123, 124.

1. In English the Hebrew word *chesed* is also translated 'mercy'. He keeps His promises to His Chosen People. God shows that He has kept His promise by protecting His People and guiding them (19.19).

2. The word *chesed* is especially used when the writer is thinking that God shows this 'steadfast love' even when His People have failed to keep their promises to Him and have disobeyed Him. In this way the word is like the New Testament word 'grace'.

Visit
References: 21.1; 50.24, 25.
Notes: pp. 63, 123, 151.

When we read in the Bible that God 'visited' His people, it means that He was in communication with them for a special purpose. Sometimes the word means that He 'visited in order to save', as in 21.1 and 50.24, and in the Song of Zechariah in Luke 1.68. Sometimes it means that He 'visited in order to punish', as in Isa. 29.6.

When God meets us, the result is a change for us. The response which we make to the meeting decides what kind of change it will be.

Key to Questions

Introduction
1. See para. 'The Authors', lines 1–11, p. 1.
2. See para. 'the Two Parts', 1, 2, 3.
3. (a) See 'Other Opinions', lines 14–21.
   (b) See 'Other Opinions', lines 22–26.
   (c) See 'Other Opinions', last 10 lines, p. 3.
4. See 'the Twentieth Century', lines 7–13.
5. See 'Our Use of Genesis', lines 1–9, and last line, p. 4.

Genesis 1.1–25
1. See Note on 1.2b.
2. See Interpretation, part 2, p. 5.
4. (a) There is repetition, as there is in a service of worship.
   (b) See p. 7, lines 1–5.
5. Psalm 8, vv. 1, 3, 4, 6, 9 and others.
   Psalm 104, vv. 1–4, 24, 27–30 and others.
   Psalm 136, vv. 1–3 and others.
6. (a) The Spirit of God is given to us.
   (b) and (c) God is still creating now.
9. See Note 'Plants' on v. 11, pp. 9 and 10.

Genesis 1.26—2.4a
1. See 1 (a) and (b), and Note on 1.26a, p. 12.
2. See last part of Note on 1.26a.
3. See Note on 1.26b, lines 1–10.
4. (a) See p. 13, last 5 lines, and p. 15, lines 1–5.
   (b) See p. 15, lines 8–23.
5. See Note on 1.27, lines 8–10, p. 15.
6. See Note on 2.2, lines 10–14, p. 18.
7. (a) and (d) They are partners, each honouring the other.
   (b) and (c) The man is head, the woman is subject to him.
8. See p. 15, lines 22–30.

Special Note A
1. See Note on p. 20, lines 1–12.
2. See Note 1 on p. 20.
3. See Note 2a on p. 20.
4. See p. 21, Note 1.
5. (a) See p. 21, Note 2.

Genesis 2.4b—2.14
1. (a) See Note on v. 7c.

2. (a) See Interpretation, Note 1, p. 22.
   (b) See Interpretation, Note 2.
3. (a) See Note on 2.9.   (b) See Note on 2.9, last 4 lines.
4. For example 'said'.
5. Genesis 3.19 and Job 10.9 point to (a).   Other passages point to (b).

Genesis 2.15—2.25
1. See Note on 2.18b, p. 28.
2. See Note on v. 15, first part, p. 26.
4. See Note on v. 20, p. 28.
5. Wisdom 2.23–24, Rom. 5.12, 1 Cor. 15.21.
6. (a) That God intended a man and a woman to be joined in marriage.
   (b) That in marriage they become 'one flesh'.
7. (a) One reason is that some people are over-working, so that there is less work for others. Also, by using machines, a few people can do work which was once done by many.

Genesis 3.1–13
1. See Note (b) on 3.1.
2. See Note on 3.7, p. 34, last few lines.
3. For example: 'said' (v. 9), 'called' (v. 9), 'clothed' (v. 21), 'sent forth' (v. 23).
4. See v. 8.
5. (a) Cain was shown that he was indeed his brother's keeper.
   (b) Elijah learnt that he was not alone and that there was work for him to do.
   (c) Job learnt that he had no right to question God.
   (d) Isaiah learnt that God had special work for him to do.
   (e) Ezekiel learnt that God could put new spirit into the people.
   (f) Paul learnt that when he persecuted people he was persecuting Jesus.

Genesis 3.14–24
1. Because God alone is Creator, and He alone knows His purpose.
2. (a) See Note on 3.16b, lines 1–6, and on 3.15 and 3.17.
3. (a) See Note on 3.16b.   (b) See Note on 3.16b, last 4 lines.
4. (a) Sarah: her son Isaac became one of the great patriarchs.
      Hannah: her son was the great prophet Samuel.
      Mary: her son was Jesus.
      Elizabeth: her son was John the Baptist.

Special Note B
1. See p. 40, lines 1–11.   2. See p. 41, lines 1–6.
3. (a) (ii)   (b) (i).   4. Exodus, Leviticus, Numbers.

165

Genesis 4.1–15
1. (a) (ii) (b) (i) (c) (i) (d) (i) and (ii) (e) (ii) (f) (ii) (g) (ii).
2. See p. 42, Outline lines 1 and 2.
3. See Outline lines 3 and 4.
4. (a) See Note on 4.15, lines 1–5. (b) See Note on 4.15, lines 7–9.
5. (a) As thanksgiving. (b) To complete a covenant.
   (c) To ask for forgiveness. (d) As a thanksgiving.
6. In 4.9 Cain says that he was not his brother's keeper.
   In Gen 1.26, God created all human beings equally in His image,
   and so as brothers. In 1 Cor. 12.26 Paul says that we all belong
   together.
7. That Abel deserved God's approval by the way in which he
   sacrificed, and that we must avoid the sin which Cain committed
   because he was evil.
8. (a) vv. 12–14.

Genesis 4.16–24
1. See Interpretation, lines 1–5.
2. (a) vv. 17, 22. (b) vv. 17, 19, 21, 25.
3. In 4.16b we read that Cain was separated from God. But according
   to Psalm 139.8 no-one can be totally separated from God.
4. (a) See Notes 1 and 3 on 4.24.
   (b) When we believe that God has forgiven us, then we are ready
   to forgive other people.
6. See Note on 4.17.

Genesis 4.25—5.32
1. See Interpretation, lines 1–4, p. 48.
2. See Note on 5.27, numbered para. 2.
3. Gen. 1.26. 5. See Note on 5.27.

Genesis 6.1–4
1. See Interpretation, numbered para. 2.
2. In 6.2 the words mean 'half-gods'; in Rom. 8.14 they mean those
   who are led by God's Spirit.

Genesis 6.5–10
1. See Interpretation, numbered para. 5.
2. (a) Human beings are sinful. (b) God is compassionate.
   (c) When we sin we are punished. (d) We can depend on God.
3. (b) See Note on 6.7a, para. 2.

Genesis 6.11—8.20
1. See Outline, lines 4–9, p. 57. 2. See 6.14. 3. See 6.18–20.
4. (a) See 8.8. (b) See 8.10–12. 5. Iraq. 6. See 8.20.

7. (a) and (b) See Note on 7.2a.
8. (a) Gen. 6, vv. 11, 12, 13, 17, Gen. 7. vv. 4.19–24.
   (b) Eleven.   (c) 45.   (d) God rescuing Noah.
9. (a) iii   (b) i   (c) i   (d) ii   (e) iii   (f) ii.
10. Be ready for times of testing.
11. (a) ii   (b) i   (c) ii   (d) i   (e) ii   (f) ii.
12. See Note on 7.19, p. 61.
13. (a) See Note on 6.14.

Genesis 8.21—9.17

1. 'Expectation' gives a better meaning, because God made a promise in His covenant. 'Contract' is not such a good word here because it is usually between two equal groups.
2. See Interpretation, numbered para. 1, p. 63.
3. (a) Said (9.1), bow (9.13), remember (9.15–16).
4. See 9.10 and 11.   5. See 9.13.   6. See 9.11.
7. (a) God will make a *new* covenant, and put His law *within* His people.
   (b) The shedding of His blood is the sign of the covenant.
   (c) Jesus said that the covenant was a new one.
8. (a) (i) David.   (ii) That David would have children who would build a 'house'.
   (iii) David had a son who built the Temple.
   (b) (i) Jesus' disciples.   (ii) He would send His Holy Spirit.
   (iii) The Spirit was received at Pentecost.
9. (a) Through Isaiah, God offered the people a time in which to repent.
   (b) Through Hosea God assured the people of His great love for them.
   (c) In the Coming of Jesus.   (d) By the sending of the Spirit.
10. (a) Those who are baptised make promises, just as God has promised to guide them.   (b) Because adults make promises 'on behalf of the baby'.
11. See 9.11.

Genesis 9.18–29

1. See Interpretation, para. 1 (c), p. 68.   2. 9.26, 27. Canaanites were excluded.
3. See Interpretation, para. 1 (b).   4. See Interpretation, para. 2 (d).
5. See Interpretation, para. 2 (a).
6. (a) That he can start again with God's help if he admits his weakness.
   (b) *Either* that people often do wrong because they are afraid, *or*

that people (like Peter) can serve God well although they have done wrong in the past.

Genesis 10.1–32
1. See Outline, last para., p. 70.
3. Isaiah 42, e.g. v. 6 or 7; Acts 17, e.g. v. 26 or 27; Rev. 7, e.g. v. 9 or 10.

Genesis 11.1–9
1. See Outline, Note on 5–9, p. 73. 2. (a) and (b) See Note on 11.1.
3. See Gen. 11.8. 4. See Interpretation, last 4 lines.
5. 'Thinking that they knew as much as God knows', 'being as God', 'being like God Himself', 'independent of God', 'on a level with God', 'having no authority except yourselves', 'as if we were God'.

Genesis 11.10–32
1. See Interpretation, lines 1, 2.
2. (a) 1. Saul. 2. Because Samuel said that God had chosen him. 3. To be king.
   (b) 1. Mary. 2. Because an angel told her. 3. To be mother of God's Son.
   (c) 1. The disciples. 2. Because Jesus chose them. 3. To 'bear fruit' and to love one another.

Special Note C
1. See p. 81, lines 7–9. 2. See p. 78, numbered para. 2.

Genesis 12.1–4a
1. (a) After the flood. (b) When He sent Abraham into a new country.
   (c) Isaac. (d) Praise.
2. See Interpretation, lines 3–8.
3. Because it was dangerous to travel far. 4. Iraq.
5. God takes the first step and calls on us to follow. 6. Obedience.
7. Exod. 3.6–11 (a) Moses. (b) To go to Pharoah. (c) He obeyed. Mark 2.13, 14 (a) Levi. (b) Follow Jesus. (c) He did follow Jesus. Acts 9.3–8 (a) Paul. (b) Go into the city of Damascus. (c) He allowed himself to be taken into the city.

Genesis 12.4b—14.24
1. (a) Gen. 2.20. (b) John 1.42. (c) Psalm 90.2.
2. (a) See Outline, p. 86, line 12. (b) See Outline, line 13.
   (c) See Outline, Note on Gen. 13.
3. See Interpretation, line 8. 4. See Note on p. 87, on 12.6.
5. To give them a land to live in. 6. See Note 2 on 14.18.

8. (a) See Note on 14.18, last 7 lines.

Genesis 15, 16, 17
1. Agreement, bond, pact.   2. See Interpretation, p. 92, lines 1–6.
3. See Note on 15.18, lines 1–5.   4. See Note on 15.6, lines 1–5.
5. That it is a matter concerning a person's heart and will.
6. (a) See Note on 16.3, last part.   7. See Additional Note, 'Say', para. 1, p. 162.

Genesis 18 and 19
1. Gen. 18.30 (a) The people of Sodom.   (b) Their sin was very 'grave' (v. 20).   (c) Their city was destroyed (19.25).
Matt. 3.7–10 (a) Some of the Pharisees and Sadducees. (b) They think that because Abraham was their 'father' they do not need to repent.   (c) There will be suffering (v. 10).
2. See 18.10.
3. In both passages we read of God being active.
4. (a) Intercession.   (b) Asking for himself.
5. (a) See Interpretation, lines 9–12, p. 95.

Genesis 20 and 21
1. See Gen. 21.14–18.
2. See Note on 21.13, p. 100, last 6 lines. God cares for everyone, not only for His Chosen People.
3. Luke 13.1–5 and John 9.1–3. No, not all disasters are sent by God as a punishment.
4. See 21.5.   6. See Note on 20.5, lines 1–4.

Genesis 22
1. See Note on 22.1b, p. 103.   2. See Interpretation, lines 1–5.
3. See Gen. 22.7.   4. See Gen. 22.14.
5. (a) and (b) See p. 101, last few lines.
6. See p. 103, lines 7–12.
9. See Interpretation, numbered para. 1, last 6 lines.

Genesis 23.1—25.18
1. See Interpretation, lines 4–8, p. 105.   2. See Note on 24.4, lines 6–9.
3. In these events they asked for God's guidance, and they received it.
4. See Interpretation, 'Note', p. 105.
5. See Note on 24.14, last 4 lines.

Genesis 25.19–34
1. and 2. See Outline, p. 108, Note on vv. 27–34.
3. See Interpretation, numbered para. 2.
4. See Note on 25.22b, p. 109.

Genesis 26.1—28.9

1. (a) 26.24 and 28.14: To be the father of many generations.
   27.27–9: To be rich and to lord it over others.
   (b) 1 Kgs. 3.5–9: An understanding mind.
   Matt. 5.3–12: See the second half of each verse.
   Eph. 1.3, 4: To be a holy person.
2. See 27.1–4.   3. See Interpretation, p. 111.
4. Nathaniel was 'someone in whom there is no guile' (John 1.47);
   Jacob was deceitful.
5. That cursing from outside us cannot harm us.

Genesis 28.10–22

1. (b) Reverence.   2. See Outline, p. 114, line 2.
3. (a) See Interpretation, last 8 lines.   (b) See Outline, last 4 lines.
4. For Jacob's vow, see Interpretation, lines 4–6. For Jesus' prayer
   see end of Mark 14.36.
5. (a) Jesus had been with them all the time, but they did not know.
   (b) Jesus was their 'bread of life', but they did not know.
7. (a) God showed Jacob and Peter how He wanted them to live, and
   showed it through their dreams.

Genesis 29.1—32.2

1. See 29, vv. 18–20.
2. For Laban's trick, see 29.21–23.
   For Jacob's trick, see Outline, Note on 30.25—31.21, lines 5–10,
   p. 118.
3. See 31.52.
4. For example, see 29.21–25 and Interpretation, last 2 lines.
5. (a) i   (b) ii   (c) i.

Genesis 32.3–32

2. See Outline, p. 122, lines 2, 3.
3. See 32, vv. 9, 13, 22.
4. Someone wrestling with him, his thigh being put out of joint, his
   receiving a new name, Israel.
5. See p. 123, lines 7, 8.   6. i, iii, iv, v, vi.
7. (a) See Note (a) at the end of Interpretation.
   (b) Asking God to 'come' does not mean that God was absent
   before we prayed. It means that we are opening ourselves to
   His presence.
10. In both experiences Jacob knew that God was present with him in a
    special way.

Genesis 33.1—37.1

1. (a) See Gen. 27.18, 19.   (b) See 33.10.   (c) See 33.11.

2. See p. 126, lines 3–5.
3. (a) In both passages believers have to live *in* the world and yet be different from unbelievers. See Note on 34.9.
   (b) Believers must not copy unbelievers.
4. (a) For example, both *want* reconciliation, as Jacob and Esau did.

Special Note D
1. See the Special Note, lines 7–11. 2. See p. 129, line 17.
3. See p. 129, last 5 lines. 4. See p. 131, lines 7–12.

Genesis 37.2—38.30
1. See Note on 37.35, p. 132. 2. See Outline, lines 3–7.
3. (a) See Interpretation, last 2 lines. (b) See Note on 37.35, lines 1–5.
4. Many people who are hated or despised by the world can serve God in a special way.
5. In the New Testament passages we read of hope of life after death; but in Gen. 37 and Psalm 6, no such hope is expressed.

Genesis 39, 40, 41
2. (a) See Outline, p. 134, lines 2–5.
   (b) See p. 134, last 4 lines.
3. (a) See Gen. 41.47–49. (b) See Gen. 40, vv. 9, 12, 21.
4. Joseph's imprisonment, and his release.
5. (i) God's presence with human beings.
   (ii) (a) Isaac. (b) Jacob. (c) Joseph. (d) Joseph. (e) Samuel. (f) David.
6. (a) False. (b) True. (c) True.

Genesis 42–45
1. (a) See Additional Note, 'Remnant', p. 160, para. 3a. (b) See para. 3b, p. 60.
   (c) The people of Israel. (d) Those who, through God's grace, are believers.
2. See Gen. 42.1, 2. 3. (a) and (b) See 43, vv. 29, 34.
4. Reverence.
5. Jesus was present, but they did not recognise Him.
   Joseph was with them, but they did not recognise him.
6. Joseph forgave his brothers. God can forgive us.

Genesis 46–48
1. (a) See Acts 13, vv. 16, 17. (b) See Additional Note, 'People of God', 2c, p. 159.
   (c) See Additional Note, 'People of God', 2d. (d) See Additional Note, 'People of God', 4.

2. See Gen. 45.16–18; 45.28; 47.4.
3. See Gen. 46.30.
4. (a) See Gen. 47.13, 14.   (b) See Gen. 37.2; 39.3–6; 41.33–36.
5. The Exodus from Egypt.

Special Note E
2. See Note E, para. 4.
3. (a) (i) See Gen. 37.23; 39.20.   (ii) See Gen. 50.20.
   (b) See Note E, last 6 lines.   (c) See Note E, last 3 lines.
   (d) See Phil. 1.12–14.

Genesis 49 and 50
1. See Interpretation, numbered paras. 1 and 2.   2. See 50.15–19.
3. To bring peace to the dead person.
4. Because Joseph had 'faith' he predicted that God would bring the Israelites out of Egypt.
5. (a) (i) Joseph's descendants.   (ii) Salvation.
   (b) (i) Israelites who made gods out of gold.   (ii) Punishment.
   (c) (i) Hannah.   (ii) Salvation.
   (d) (i) 'Other lords', i.e. foreigners.   (ii) Punishment.
   (e) (i) Gentiles.   (ii) Salvation.
6. There is temptation for human beings to behave as if they were God.

Index

This Index includes only the more important proper names of people and places, and the main subjects which occur in the Book of Genesis, or which are discussed in the Study Guide.

173

The Society for Promoting Christian Knowledge (SPCK) was founded in 1698. It has as its purpose three main tasks:

- **Communicating the Christian faith in its rich diversity**
- **Helping people to understand the Christian faith and to develop their personal faith**
- **Equipping Christians for mission and ministry**

SPCK Worldwide serves the Church through Christian literature and communication projects in over 100 countries. Special schemes also provide books for those training for ministry in many parts of the developing world. SPCK Worldwide's ministry involves Churches of many traditions. This worldwide service depends upon the generosity of others and all gifts are spent wholly on ministry programmes, without deductions.

SPCK Bookshops support the life of the Christian community by making available a full range of Christian literature and other resources, and by providing support to bookstalls and book agents throughout the UK. SPCK Bookshops' mail order department meets the needs of overseas customers and those unable to have access to local bookshops.

SPCK Publishing produces Christian books and resources, covering a wide range of inspirational, pastoral, practical and academic subjects. Authors are drawn from many different Christian traditions, and publications aim to meet the needs of a wide variety of readers in the UK and throughout the world.

The Society does not necessarily endorse the individual views contained in its publications, but hopes they stimulate readers to think about and further develop their Christian faith.

For further information about the Society, please write to:
SPCK, Holy Trinity Church, Marylebone Road,
London NW1 4DU, United Kingdom.
Telephone: 0171 387 5282